英語対訳で旅する東京
楽しく歩ける！楽々わかる！

ブルーガイド編集部 編

Jon Morris 英文翻訳

J JIPPI Compact

実業之日本社

Introduction

Tokyo attracts many tourists from all over the world. It is a place that brings together all the attractions and interest of Japan, from the cutting edge of fashion to the Japanese culture of the good old days.

This book introduces Japan's number one tourist destination in Japanese with English translation. The original Japanese text was prepared by the *Burū Gaido* editorial staff, travel guidebook professionals. It is designed to be useful for those who wish to understand the guide articles in English, use the English versions of the guide articles to explore Tokyo themselves, and those who would like to try guiding foreign travelers around Tokyo in English.

We have used simple English wherever possible in our guidebook-style introductions to the major famous and historical spots. To make the text easier to understand, we have numbered the English sentences to match the corresponding sentences in the Japanese text. We have also underlined key English words and phrases and given their Japanese equivalents in superscript.

"This is how you introduce one of the long-established stores in *Ginza*!" "So that's the phrase for the *Roppongi* neighborhood"-enjoy reading about Tokyo along with the matched translations. We hope this book will help you get to know Tokyo, and explore it!

PREFACE / はじめに

はじめに

　世界中からたくさんの外国人観光客が集まる、東京。流行の最先端から古き良き日本文化まで、まさに日本の魅力が凝縮した街といえます。

　本書はそんな日本一の観光都市・東京を、日本語と英語の対訳で紹介する一冊です。日本語の原文は、旅行ガイドブックを制作するブルーガイド編集部によるもので、ガイド記事を英語で理解したい人、それを基に実際に歩いてみたい人、さらに外国人の旅行者を英語で案内してみたい人それぞれに向けて、役立つつくりとなっています。

　本書ではなるべく平易な英語を用いて、見どころを中心に主に旅行ガイドブックでとりあげられる物件を紹介しています。英文と和訳文に相番号を付けて対応させたり、要所の英単語や熟語に下線を引いて日本語訳をつけるなどして、理解しやすくしています。

　「銀座の老舗は、こんな風に紹介するんだ！」「六本木界隈の散策は、英語でこう表現するんだ！」などと、対訳の表現を楽しみながら東京を読んで、知って、巡ってもらえると幸いです。

第1章 東京とはどんなところ？ / What is Tokyo ?

1	東京の成り立ちと歴史 / The origins and history of Tokyo	12
2	東京の街の特徴（1）/ The distinctive features of Tokyo (1)	14
3	東京の街の特徴（2）/ The distinctive features of Tokyo (2)	16
4	東京の食事情 / Tokyo's food culture	18
5	東京の買い物事情 / Tokyo's shopping culture	20
6	東京の交通事情 / Transportation in Tokyo	22

■旅のポイント・お得な切符で東京を散歩する
　　　　　　　　　　　　　　/ Discount tickets for Tokyo travel　24

第2章　東京中心部 / Central Tokyo

7	エリアガイド　銀座 / *Ginza*	26
8	銀座の老舗：資生堂パーラー銀座本店 / The long-established stores of *Ginza* : *Shiseidō* Parlour *Ginza*	28
9	銀座の老舗：東京鳩居堂 / The long-established stores of *Ginza* : Tokyo *Kyūkyo-dō*	29
10	歌舞伎座 / *Kabuki-za*	30

■旅のポイント・銀座八丁神社巡り
　　　　　　　　　　　　　　/ Visiting the shrines in *Ginza Hacchō*　32

11	エリアガイド　築地 / *Tsukiji*	34
12	築地場内市場 / The *Tsukiji* Inner Market	36
13	築地場外市場 / The *Tsukiji* Outer Market	37

■旅のポイント・寿司 / Sushi　38

14	エリアガイド　新橋 / *Shimbashi*	40

■旅のポイント・居酒屋 / *Izakaya* (Japanese-style bars)　42

15	エリアガイド　日本橋 / *Nihombashi*	44

CONTENTS / **目次**

16	日本橋髙島屋 / *Nihombashi Takashimaya*	46
17	たいめいけん / *Taimeiken*	47
18	エリアガイド　丸の内 / *Marunouchi*	48
19	東京駅丸の内駅舎 / Tokyo Station, *Marunouchi* Station Building	50
20	三菱一号館 / *Mitsubishi Ichigōkan* Building	52
21	明治生命館 / *Meiji Seimei-kan* Building	53
22	エリアガイド　皇居 / The Imperial Palace	54
23	日比谷公園 / *Hibiya* Park	56
24	国会議事堂 / The Diet Building	57
■旅のポイント・東京みやげ / Tokyo Souvenirs		58

第3章　東京下町 / Traditional Tokyo

25	エリアガイド　浅草 / *Asakusa*	60
26	浅草寺 / *Sensō-ji* temple	62
27	仲見世 / *Nakamise*	64
28	浅草花やしき / *Asakusa Hanayashiki*	66
29	浅草演芸ホール / The *Asakusa Engei* Hall	67
30	浅草の老舗：神谷バー / Old shops in *Asakusa* : The *Kamiya* Bar	68
31	浅草の老舗：やげん堀 / Old shops in *Asakusa* : *Yagembori*	69
32	かっぱ橋道具街 / The *Kappa-bashi* utensils street	70
■旅のポイント・下町伝統の味・どぜう料理　　　　　　　　／ The taste of *Shitamachi* : loach cuisine		72
■旅のポイント・江戸の老舗のそばを味わう　　　　　　　　／ The taste of *Edo*-style *soba*		73
33	東京スカイツリー / Tokyo Skytree	74
■旅のポイント・水上バスで下町さんぽ　　　　　　　　／ A trip through *Shitamachi* by water bus		76

34	エリアガイド　両国 / Ryōgoku	78
35	両国国技館 / Ryōgoku Kokugikan	80
36	江戸東京博物館 / The Edo-Tokyo Museum	82
37	エリアガイド　上野 / Ueno	84
38	上野恩賜公園 / Ueno Onshi Park	86
39	上野動物園 / Ueno Zoo	88
40	東京国立博物館 / The Tokyo National Museum	89
41	国立科学博物館 / The National Science Museum	90
42	国立西洋美術館 / The National Museum of Western Arts	91
43	横山大観記念館 / Yokoyama Taikan Memorial Hall	92
44	台東区立下町風俗資料館 / The Shitamachi Museum	93
45	アメ横 / Ameyoko	94
46	湯島天満宮 / Yushima Temman-gū shrine	96
47	旧岩崎邸庭園 / Kyū-Iwasaki-tei Garden	97
48	エリアガイド　谷根千 / Yanesen	98
49	根津神社 / Nezu Jinja shrine	100
■旅のポイント・夕焼けだんだんと谷中銀座商店街		
	/ Yūyake Dandan and the Yanaka-ginza shopping street	101
50	エリアガイド　秋葉原 / Akihabara	102
51	秋葉原ラジオセンター / Akihabara Radio Center	104
■旅のポイント・オタクの聖地 / Holy ground for otaku culture		105
52	エリアガイド　神田・神保町 / Kanda, Jimbōchō	106
53	いせ源 / Isegen	108
54	竹むら / Takemura	109
■旅のポイント・銭湯でゆったりくつろぐ		
	/ Relaxing at a sentō bathhouse	110

第4章　東京の繁華街 / Downtown Tokyo

55	エリアガイド　お台場 / *Odaiba*	112
56	大江戸温泉物語 / *Ōedo Onsen Monogatari*	114
57	日本科学未来館 / *Miraikan* (National Museum of Emerging Science and Innovation)	115
58	レインボーブリッジ / Rainbow Bridge	116
■旅のポイント・ゆりかもめ / *Yurikamome*		117
59	エリアガイド　六本木 / *Roppongi*	118
60	六本木ヒルズ / *Roppongi* Hills	120
61	東京ミッドタウン / Tokyo Midtown	122
62	東京タワー / Tokyo Tower	124
63	エリアガイド　麻布十番 / *Azabu Jūban*	126
■旅のポイント・六本木の美術館巡り / Visiting the art museums of *Roppongi*		128
64	エリアガイド　新宿 / *Shinjuku*	130
65	都庁と西口高層ビル群 / The Tokyo Metropolitan Government Office and the high-rise buildings of the west gate	132
66	ゴールデン街 / Golden District	134
67	思い出横丁 / *Omoide Yokochō*	135
68	新宿御苑 / *Shinjuku* Imperial Garden	136
69	新宿末廣亭 / *Shinjuku Suehirotei*	137
70	エリアガイド　新大久保 / *Shin-Ōkubo*	138
71	エリアガイド　神楽坂 / *Kagurazaka*	140
72	エリアガイド　渋谷 / *Shibuya*	142
73	渋谷駅ハチ公口前広場 / *Shibuya* Station *Hachikō* Square	144
74	SHIBUYA109 / *SHIBUYA*109	146
75	渋谷ヒカリエ / *Shibuya Hikarie*	147
76	エリアガイド　表参道 / *Omotesandō*	148
77	明治神宮 / *Meiji Jingū* shrine	150

CONTENTS / 目次

78	表参道ヒルズ / Omotesandō Hills	151
79	エリアガイド　原宿 / Harajuku	152
80	竹下通り / Takeshita-dōri Street	154
■旅のポイント・能楽 / Nō plays		156
81	エリアガイド　恵比寿・代官山 / Ebisu, Daikan'yama	158
82	恵比寿ガーデンプレイス / Yebisu Garden Place	160
83	エリアガイド　吉祥寺 / Kichijōji	162
84	井の頭恩賜公園 / Inokashira Onshi Park	164
85	ハモニカ横丁 / Harmonica Yokochō	166
86	アトレ吉祥寺・キラリナ吉祥寺 / Atre Kichijōji, Kirarina Kichijōji	167

地図・東京広域地図	168
地図・東京中心部	170
東京の鉄道・地下鉄路線図	172

装丁／杉本欣右
DTP・地図製作／㈱千秋社
英文編集／テクスタイド
日本文編集／ブルーガイド編集部

※日本語の原文は、主にブルーガイドてくてく歩き４「東京」、「東京おさんぽマップ」「東京下町おさんぽマップ」の記事をもとに、加筆しています。内容は2014年９月現在のものです。
※英文中の日本語表記について、日本語（人名・地名など）は原則的にヘボン式ローマ字とし、イタリック体で表記しています。また、長音の母音の上には横棒をつけています。

Chapter 1

What is Tokyo ?

第1章
東京とはどんなところ？

1 The origins and history of Tokyo

①In 1603, with the foundation of the *Tokugawa* Shogunate, *Edo* (later Tokyo) suddenly took the center stage in Japanese history. Over 10,000 years ago, during the early *Jōmon* period, much of what is now Tokyo was at the bottom of the sea. The cliff that runs along part of the west side of the current JR *Keihin Tōhoku* Line between *Ueno* and *Akabane* is the coastline as it was at that time.

②In the mid-15th century, with Japan in the Warring States (*Sengoku*) period, *Ōta Dōkan* built *Edo* castle. In 1590, *Toyotomi Hideyoshi* had *Tokugawa Ieyasu* relocate to the *Kantō* Region, enter *Edo*, and complete the founding of a city that was to become the heart of the *Edo* shogunate. *Edo*, the *Tokugawa* shogun's center of power, continued to prosper for the next 300 years.

③In 1868, at the time of the *Meiji* Restoration, *Edo*'s name was changed to Tokyo. The Imperial Palace, the residence

第1章●東京とはどんなところ?

of the Emperor, was moved from *Kyōto* to Tokyo, and
　　　天皇
Tokyo became the capital of Japan in both name and fact.
　　　　　　　　　　　　　　　　　　　　名実ともに

1. 東京の成り立ちと歴史

①1603(慶長8)年、徳川幕府が開かれたことにより、一躍日本史の表舞台に登場した江戸・東京。1万年ほど前の縄文時代前期には、東京のかなりの部分が海の底でした。今のJR京浜東北線の上野~赤羽間などの、線路沿い西側の一部が崖になっているのはその頃の海岸線です。

②戦国時代に入る15世紀半ば、太田道灌が江戸城を築きました。1590(天正18)年、豊臣秀吉により徳川家康が関東に移封されて江戸に入り、江戸幕府につながる街の基礎を造り上げました。そして以後300年間、江戸は徳川幕府の中心地として、繁栄の一途をたどります。

③1868(慶応4=明治元)年、明治維新により江戸は東京と名を改められます。天皇の居所である御所が京都から東京に移され、名実ともに日本の都、つまり首都となりました。

2 The distinctive features of Tokyo (1)

①Tokyo stretches many miles east to west. From Mt. *Kumotori* in the west, Tokyo's highest peak (最高峰), to the areas along the shore (沿岸) of Tokyo Bay (東京湾) and the low-lying areas (低地帯) along *Edo-gawa* River in the east. Its terrain, with an elevation difference (標高差) of over 2000 meters, is rich in variety (バラエティに富む).

②Tokyo's core is a traditional area that includes such places as *Kanda*, *Nihombashi*, and *Ginza*. It developed radiating outward (放射状に広がる) along the *Gokaidō*, the five highways of *Tōkaidō*, *Nakasendō*, *Nikkō Dōchū*, *Ōshū Dōchū*, and *Kōshū Dōchū* that connected the old post towns (旧宿場町) where people could stop on their travels. By putting together (重ね合わせる) with this the circular JR *Yamanote* Line (JR山手線) and the JR *Chūō* Line (JR中央線) which crosses east to west on this area with this. Tokyo may be roughly (おおよそ) divided into four areas.

③The northeast area includes places such as *Akihabara*, *Ueno* and *Asakusa*, and is an area that has developed over

many years. On the other hand, the northwest area which
時間をかけて
includes *Nakano*, *Kōenji*, and *Kichijōji* is land that has
been developed from farming villages into residential areas
　　　　　　　　　　　　　農村　　　　　　　　住宅地
from the *Meiji* period onward, and you can see vegetable
　　　　明治時代　　　〜以降　　　　　　　　　　　野菜畑
fields and orchards around this area even now.
　　　　　　果樹園

2. 東京の街の特徴（1）

①東西に長い東京。西は東京都最高峰の雲取山（くもとりやま）から、東は東京湾沿岸と江戸川沿いの低地帯まで、標高差2000mを超えるバラエティに富んだ地形をしています。

②東京は神田・日本橋・銀座などを含む下町を核として、江戸時代に整備された「五街道」の東海道（とうかいどう）・中山道（なかせんどう）・日光道中（にっこうどうちゅう）・奥州道中（おうしゅうどうちゅう）・甲州道中（こうしゅうどうちゅう）の旧宿場町をつないで放射状に発展しました。これに環状のJR山手線と東西に横断するJR中央線を重ね合わせると、おおよそ4つのエリアに分けられます。

③北東部は秋葉原・上野・浅草などを含む古くから発展した街です。また、北西部の中野・高円寺・吉祥寺などは明治以降に農村から住宅地として開けた地域で、現在でもところどころに野菜畑や果樹園を見受けることがあります。

3 The distinctive features of Tokyo (2)

①From *Shinjuku* southward, the southwest area of Tokyo which includes *Shibuya* and *Aoyama* developed from the *Meiji* period onward, particularly after the war, into a district that is popular with young people. The southeast area has been the site of new town planning, carried out as part of Japan's economic development. The *Den'enchōfu* 'garden city' area is representative of these new developments.

②Moving northward along the *Yamanote* Line with Tokyo Station as your starting point, you can enjoy a Tokyo that is brimming with traditional charm. The neighborhood between *Nihombashi* and *Ginza* has many long-established shops dating to the *Edo* period, and the neighborhoods of *Ueno* and *Asakusa* have a folksy atmosphere.

③There is also *Kagurazaka*, where the atmosphere of the old *geisha* district of *Edo* still remains. There is the book district of *Kanda*'s *Jimbō-chō*, and *Roppongi*, the fashionable art district. The entire area of *Odaiba* is like one big amusement facility. Find the Tokyo that suits you best from among these unique areas.

アミューズメント施設 　　　　　　　　一番合う
個性的な

3. 東京の街の特徴（２）

①新宿以南、南西部の渋谷・青山などは明治以降、特に戦後に発展した若者に人気のある街ということになります。そこから南東部にかけては田園調布に代表されるように、日本の経済的発展に伴い新しい街づくりも行われました。
②東京駅を基点に山手線で北上すると、下町風情あふれる東京を楽しめます。江戸時代からの老舗が多い日本橋〜銀座界隈、庶民的な味わいがあるのは上野、浅草界隈。
③ほかにも江戸の花街風情が残る神楽坂。本の街、神田・神保町。おしゃれなアートの街、六本木。街全体がアミューズメント施設のようなお台場。これら個性的な街から、好みの東京を見つけてみては？

4 Tokyo's food culture

①Say *Edomae* (*Edo* style) and the first thing that comes to mind is *sushi*. Its origins lie with the fact that the fresh seafood available at *Edominato* harbor was called *Edomae*. *Soba* (buckwheat noodles) also offer a taste of the lifestyle of the common folk of *Edo*. It is said that at the end of the *Edo* period, there were over 3000 *soba* shops here.

②Restaurants such as *Ginza*'s *Renga-tei*, founded in 1895, arranged Western-style dishes to suit Japanese tastes and helped expand Western-style cuisine. *Tonkatsu* (fried pork cutlets) were already a meal enjoyed by the general populace of Tokyo by the late *Meiji* period.

③These days, it is safe to say that there is no cuisine from around the country or around the world that you can't enjoy in Tokyo. In *Ginza*, there is a wide variety of restaurants from the expensive places to those serving everyday meals to the general populace. If you prefer fashionable

French or Italian restaurants, you should go to the *Aoyama*, *Omotesandō*, and *Daikanyama* area. Small and unique restaurants serving Japanese and Western-style cuisine are popular in *Kagurazaka*.

個性的な

4. 東京の食事情

①江戸前といえば寿司。江戸湊でとれる新鮮な魚介類が、江戸前と呼ばれたのが始まりです。また蕎麦も江戸の庶民の味です。江戸時代末には3000軒以上の蕎麦屋があったともいわれます。

②洋食は1895（明治28）年創業の銀座の「煉瓦亭」などが、洋風料理をアレンジして広めていったといい、とんかつは明治時代末頃の東京では、すでに庶民の味として親しまれていました。

③現在の東京では全国各地、世界各国、味わえない料理はないといってもいいでしょう。銀座なら高級店から庶民的な店まで、幅広くそろいます。しゃれたフレンチやイタリアンがお好みなら、青山・表参道・代官山界隈へ。神楽坂は隠れ家風の個性的な和食・洋食の店で人気を集めています。

5 Tokyo's shopping culture

①For shopping in Tokyo, the first place that comes to mind [思い浮かぶ] is the area between *Ginza* and *Yūrakuchō*. Long-established [老舗] department stores such as *Wakō*, *Mitsukoshi*, and *Matsuya*, famous fast fashion [ファストファッション] shops, and a range of high-class [高級な] brand shops all line [軒を連ねる] the streets within a 30-minute walking distance [徒歩30分圏内].

②In areas where the station buildings [駅ビル] and department stores are directly connected [直結している], like *Ikebukuro* and *Shinjuku*, there is a substantial variety of merchandise [商品] for every generation, including senior citizens [シニア層]. In *Shibuya*, there are many fashion store buildings [ファッションビル], each catering for [〜を提供する] a specific fashion. This area is very popular with [〜に人気がある] young women.

③There is also a great variety of specialty store [専門店] areas. *Jimbō-chō* has its books. *Akihabara* has its hobbies and personal computers. The *Tsukiji* Outer Market [築地場外市場] and *Ueno*'s *Ameyoko* are the places to buy seafood [海産物]. The *Aoyama*,

Omotesandō, and *Harajuku* area is full of trendsetting bou-
  流行の先端の
tiques and variety shops catering to refined tastes. *Haraju-*
                                          洗練された
ku's *Takeshita-dōri* Street is a Mecca for teenage girls.
     竹下通り   メッカ(聖地)

5. 東京の買い物事情

①東京で買い物といえば、まず思い浮かぶのが銀座〜有楽町界隈。和光、三越、松屋などの老舗百貨店から有名ファストファッションの店、さらに高級ブランド各店が、歩いて30分圏内に軒を連ねています。

②駅ビルと百貨店が直結していて便利な池袋や新宿では、シニア層向けも含む幅広い世代向けの商品が充実。渋谷はビルごとに傾向が鮮明なファッションビルが多く、若い女性を中心に人気です。

③専門店街もさまざまです。本の神保町。趣味とパソコンの秋葉原。海産物なら築地場外市場や上野のアメ横。流行の先端とハイセンスなブティックや雑貨店が軒を連ねる青山〜表参道〜原宿界隈。原宿・竹下通りは10代の女の子の聖地です。

6 Transportation in Tokyo

①The basic structure of Tokyo's road system consists of the ring roads that surround the metropolitan center in concentric circles and the *Gokaidō*, the five highways of the *Edo period* which still run through it in a radial pattern like the spokes of a wheel. These are the main arteries from which spread forth many smaller roads joined to them like capillaries.

②In the same manner, Tokyo's railways center on the JR *Yamanote* Line that circles the capital and the central JR *Chūō* Line that runs crossways through it. Running north to south, there is the JR *Keihin Tōhoku* Line in the east of Tokyo and the JR *Saikyō* Line in the west. The Tokyo subway network covers the metropolitan center.

③Use the subway for exploring the center of Tokyo. There is a rich variety of different bargain day tickets on offer, so you should certainly make use of one of these. Community bus networks connecting local areas can also be used for around 100 yen per journey. 18 such bus routes are in operation, including the '*Hachikō*' bus in *Shibuya* ward, the '*Megurin*' bus in *Taitō* ward and the '*Edo* bus' in the central *Chūo* ward.

1回の乗車あたり／バス路線／操業中／渋谷区

6. 東京の交通事情

①東京の道路は同心円状に都心を取り巻く環状道路と、それを縦に貫き放射状に延びる江戸時代以来の五街道が基本構造。この大動脈を毛細血管のように広がる道が繋いでいます。

②同様に、鉄道も環状線のJR山手線とそれを東西に横断するJR中央本線が中心。さらに南北は東側にJR京浜東北線、西側にJR埼京線が走り、都心は地下鉄網が張り巡らされています。

③都心の散策には地下鉄を活用しましょう。得する一日乗車券の券種も豊富なので、利用しない手はありません。また1回100円程度の運賃で乗れ、近いエリアを結ぶコミュニティバス網も整備されています。渋谷区の「ハチ公バス」、台東区の「めぐりん」、中央区の「江戸バス」など18路線あります。

旅のポイント

Discount tickets for Tokyo travel
お得な切符で東京を散歩する

If you are going to travel around an area as wide as Tokyo, you should certainly make use of one-day unlimited travel tickets. There are tickets suitable for sightseeing available from JR, the subways, and also from private rail lines.

JR Lines and Subway Lines: 'The Tokyo One-Day Free Ticket' allows unlimited use of JR lines within the metropolitan area, the Tokyo Metro and *Toei* subway lines, *Toei* buses, the *Toden Arakawa* Line, and the *Nippori-Toneri* Liner for one day. The cost for one adult is 1590 yen (as of 2014).

Subway Lines: 'The Common One-day Ticket for the Tokyo Metro & *Toei* Subway' allows unlimited use of all of the 13 subway lines of the Tokyo Metro and *Toei* Subway. The cost for one adult is 1000 yen (as of 2014).

　広い東京を巡るなら、1日乗り降り自由の乗車券を駆使しない手はありません。JRや地下鉄のほか、私鉄各線にも観光に適した切符があります。

　JR線＋地下鉄：「東京フリーきっぷ」…首都圏内のJR線、地下鉄の東京メトロと都営地下鉄、都バス、都電、日暮里・舎人(とねり)ライナーに乗り放題。料金は大人が1590円（2014年現在）。

　地下鉄：「東京メトロ・都営地下鉄　共通一日乗車券」…東京メトロと都営地下鉄の全13路線が1日乗り放題。料金は大人が1000円（2014年現在）。

Chapter 2

Central Tokyo

第2章
東京中心部

7 AREA GUIDE

Ginza

①Many people from both inside and outside Japan visit this prominent and historical shopping district of Tokyo.
屈指の / 商店街

②Long-established department stores such as *Matsuya* and
老舗
Mitsukoshi, as well as large-scale commercial buildings,
大規模商業施設
stand along the *Ginza* Boulevard *(Chūō* Boulevard) which
銀座通り
runs through the center of this beautiful checkerboard-style
碁盤の目
district. Many shops, including some long-running and well-known ones, line the side roads.
名店 / 裏通り

③The district's name comes from a currency mint built here
〜に由来する / 鋳造所
during the *Edo* period. In the early *Meiji* period, it was
江戸時代 / 明治時代
reborn as a district of Western European-style brick buildings.
煉瓦街

④Until quite recently, there were many top-ranking brand
一流
shops and expensive restaurants here, and this area gave
高級料亭

the impression of being a place for rich people to gather. In recent years however, branches of low-cost clothing stores (低価格衣料品店) such as UNIQLO have opened here, and expensive restaurants are offering low-cost (低価格) lunches, so it is becoming a place that everyone can enjoy.

7. 銀座(ぎんざ)
エリアガイド

①東京でも屈指の歴史ある商店街として、国内外から多くの人が訪れています。
②きれいな碁盤の目の街の中心を走る、銀座通り(中央通り)に沿って、松屋(まつや)や三越(みつこし)などの老舗百貨店や大規模商業施設が建ち、裏通りにも老舗や名店など、多くの店が軒を連ねています。
③江戸時代に造られた貨幣の鋳造所が地名の由来で、明治時代に入り、西欧風の煉瓦街に生まれ変わりました。
④少し前までは、一流ブランドショップや高級料亭などが多く、お金持ちの集まる街という印象の強いエリアでしたが、近年ではユニクロなどの低価格衣料品店が出店、夜は高級な飲食店もランチに低価格のメニューを提供するなど、誰もが楽しめる街になってきています。

8. The long-established stores of *Ginza* : *Shiseidō* Parlour *Ginza*
This is the authentic taste of *Ginza* luxury

①In 1902, *Shiseidō* Parlour <u>originated as</u> the first soda foun-
　　　　　　　　　　　　　　～として始まる
tain (a store for the production and sales of soda water and

ice cream) in Japan.

②In 1928, a <u>full-scale</u> restaurant opened, and this continues
　　　　　　本格的な
to be loved as <u>a pioneer</u> of Western cuisine in Japan.
　　　　　　　　草分け
③The meat croquette that originated here in the early days

of <u>the *Shōwa* period</u>, <u>thick and creamy</u> on the inside, <u>crisp</u>
　　　昭和　　　　　　　トロトロ　　　　　　　　　　　カリッとした
on the outside, is <u>a traditional signature</u>
　　　　　　　　　伝統の味
<u>product</u> of this restaurant.

---

8. 銀座の老舗：資生堂パーラー銀座本店
これぞ高級なイメージの銀座の味

①1902（明治35）年、日本初のソーダファウンテン（ソーダ水やアイスクリームの製造・販売店）として誕生しました。
②1928（昭和３）年、本格的なレストランを開業し、西洋料理の草分け的存在として愛され続けています。
③昭和初期に発案されたミートクロケットは、中はトロトロ、外はカリッとした食感のこの店伝統の味です。

9 The long-established stores of *Ginza* : Tokyo *Kyūkyo-dō*
Unchanging Traditional Arts and Crafts of Japan

①The beginnings of this store are in 1663, when it was founded in *Kyōto* as an apothecary. From around 1700 onward, it began selling incense and supplies for paintings and calligraphy.
創立された　　　　　　　薬種商
〜以降　　　　　　　香　　　　　　書画用品

②Currently, it is known as a hallmark of specialist shop dealing in incense and Japanese stationery. Many such products, both practical and tasteful, are sold in this store.
専門店
実用的な　　趣味のよい

The displays in *Kyūkyo-dō* store offer a sense of the beauty of Japan's four seasons.

---

9. 銀座の老舗：東京鳩居堂
変わらぬ日本伝統の和雑貨

①1663（寛文3）年、京都で薬種商として創業したのが始まりです。1700（元禄13）年頃から、お香や書画用品を扱うようになりました。

②現在では、日本を代表するお香や文房具の専門店として知られ、趣味と実益を兼備した多くの商品を、日本の美しい四季を感じられる店内で販売しています。

10 *Kabuki-za*
A *kabuki* theater reborn

①The *Kabuki-za* is a theater <u>exclusively for</u> the performance of *kabuki*, a form of <u>drama</u> that is one of <u>the traditional performing arts</u> <u>original to Japan</u>.

②When it first opened in 1889, it was <u>common</u> to give names to theaters such as '*Ichimura-za*' or '*Shintomi-za*' after <u>the theater proprietor</u> or <u>a place name</u>. It was therefore very <u>innovative</u> to <u>name the theater after</u> the genre of dramatic art being performed there.

③After that, though it has faced various <u>hardships</u> such as fires, earthquakes, and <u>bombing</u> during <u>the Pacific War</u>, it has been repeatedly rebuilt, and <u>exists to this day</u> as one of the leading theaters of the nation.

④The current building, <u>the 5th</u>, <u>opened</u> in 2013. A high-rise office building towers behind it.

⑤For those who won't be <u>attending a performance</u>, and on days when no performance is put on, the *Kabuki-za* Gallery on the 5th floor of the *Kabukiza* Tower offers the opportunity to experience the world of *kabuki*. Here, special exhibitions (企画展) introducing the fascination (魅力) on *kabuki* are held, displaying items such as costumes and small props (小道具) used on stage.

10. 歌舞伎座(かぶきざ)
生まれ変わった歌舞伎の専門劇場

①日本固有の演劇で伝統芸能の一つでもある、歌舞伎の専門劇場です。

②1889（明治22）年の開場当時、劇場の名前には「市村座(いちむらざ)」「新富座(しんとみざ)」など座元の名や地名を付けるのが一般的で、演劇のジャンルをそのまま劇場の名にしたことはとても斬新でした。

③その後、火災や震災、太平洋戦争による空襲など、さまざまな困難に直面しながらも、再建を繰り返し、国を代表する劇場として今日に至っています。

④現在の建物は、2013（平成25）年にこけら落としをした5代目。後ろには高層のオフィスタワーがそびえています。

⑤休演日や観劇をしない人も、歌舞伎の世界に触れられるのが、歌舞伎座タワー5階にある歌舞伎座ギャラリー。舞台で使用された衣装や小道具の展示をはじめ、歌舞伎の面白さを紹介する企画展も行われます。

Visiting the shrines in *Ginza Hacchō*
銀座八丁神社巡り

Ginza has many shrines in unexpected places, such as on the tops of buildings or along side streets. Moreover, making a tour of the shrines scattered throughout the area from *Ginza Icchō-me* to *Ginza Hacchō-me* is said to bring you good fortune.

As *Ginza* is an area which developed as a commercial district, one of its characteristics is that there are many shrines here that offer divine blessings such as success in business, success in one's career, or success in business ventures. Shrines such as the *Ginza Shusse* (Career Advancement) *Jizōson* (dedicated to Kṣitigarbha) on the *Ginza* Terrace on the 9th floor of *Ginza Mitsukoshi*, or the *Seikō* (success) *Inari* shrine (which is usually not open to the public) located in the *Shiseidō* building show how the prayerful hopes of the people who do business in *Ginza* are included in the names of the shrines themselves.

A *Ginza Hacchō* shrine stamp rally is held during the Autumn *Ginza* event every year from late October to early November. This, along with other events, makes an enjoyable theme for walks around *Ginza* in autumn.

　銀座にはビルの屋上や路地といった意外なところに、神社がまつられています。そして銀座一丁目から八丁目までに点在する神社を巡ると福運を招くといわれています。

　商人の街として発展した銀座なので商売繁盛や出世祈願、事業成功などのご利益を掲げている神社が多いのが特徴。銀座三越9階銀座テラスの銀座出世地蔵尊や、資生堂本社に鎮座する成功稲荷神社（普段

旅のポイント

は非公開）など、神社の名前にも銀座で商売をする人たちの願いが込められています。

　毎年10月下旬〜11月上旬に開催されているイベント・オータムギンザの中で、銀座八丁神社めぐりのスタンプラリーが開催されるなど、秋の銀座歩きのテーマとして楽しまれています。

11 AREA GUIDE

Tsukiji

① The history of *Tsukiji*, the gourmet district with a fish market that feeds the metropolis of Tokyo, begins in 1657 with the Great Fire of *Meireki*. *Asakusa*'s *Nishihongan-ji* branch temple had burned down in that Great Fire, the largest blaze of the *Edo* period. The land reclaimed by filling in the estuary of the *Sumida-gawa* River in order to provide a new location for the rebuilding of the temple became known as *Tsukiji*.

② From the late *Edo* period until the Japanese Navy was dissolved at the end of the Pacific War, it was used primarily as a naval site, including places such as an area for warship drills and a military medical college.

③ The fish market in *Nihombashi* that had supported the dietary lifestyle of *Edo* and Tokyo for over 300 years was

moved to *Tsukiji* in 1935 after it burned down in the Great *Kantō* Earthquake. The initial development of the *Tsukiji*
関東大震災
Outer Market took place at this time.

11. 築地
エリアガイド

①大都市東京の食を支える魚市場のあるグルメな街・築地の歴史は、1657（明暦3）年に起きた明暦の大火に始まります。江戸時代最大のこの大火で焼失した浅草の西本願寺別院の移転のため、隅田川の河口部を埋め立てられて築かれた土地が「築地」です。

②江戸時代末期から太平洋戦争後に海軍が解体されるまでは、軍艦操練所や軍医学校など主には海軍用地として使用されていました。

③その中、300年以上にわたって江戸・東京の食生活をささえてきた日本橋の魚河岸が関東大震災で焼失、1935（昭和10）年に築地に移転し、場外にも市場が形成されていきました。

12. The *Tsukiji* Inner Market

Definitely watch the auctions-overflowing with vigor and excitement!

①The *Tsukiji* Inner Market is the largest wholesale market (卸売市場) in Japan, with 900 wholesale stores (仲卸店) inside selling marine products (水産物), fruits, and vegetables to traders.

②The areas within the market, including the auction hall (セリ場), the processing area (加工所), and the refrigeration building (冷凍庫棟), are all lively and full of energy (活力にあふれる). General consumers (一般客) who want to shop or dine (食事をする) here should please proceed to the *Uogashi Yokochō* set up in a corner of (〜の一角に) the market area.

③The inner market is scheduled to be moved to *Toyosu* in 2016.

---

12. 築地場内市場
あふれる活気と熱気　ぜひセリを見学してみよう！

①水産物と青果の仲卸店が900軒も並ぶ、日本最大の卸売市場です。

②セリ場や加工所、冷凍庫棟などがある場内は、活気にあふれています。一般客の買い物や食事は、一角に設けられた魚がし横丁へ。

③場内市場は2016（平成28）年に、豊洲に移転する予定です。

13 The *Tsukiji* Outer Market
Get inexpensive, high-quality ingredients here!

①The *Tsukiji* Outer Market brings together 400 shops in a space of <u>200 meters square</u>.
　　　　　　　　　　　　　　　　　　　　　　200m四方
②<u>In contrast with</u> the inner market which is <u>targeted</u>
　～に対して　　　　　　　　　　　　　　　　　　　～を対象にする
<u>toward</u> <u>merchants</u>, one characteristic of the outer market is
　　　　業者
that it has many shops which general consumers and tourists can also use. <u>Nonetheless</u>, you should be aware that as
　　　　　　　　　とはいえ
many of the shops, even in the outer market, <u>are patronized</u>
　　　　　　　　　　　　　　　　　　　　　　～が常客である
<u>by</u> professional <u>fish dealers</u> and <u>cooks</u>. Such shops com-
　　　　　　　　魚屋　　　　　　料理人
monly open early in the morning and close early in the afternoon.

---

13. 築地場外市場
安く良質の食材を手に入れよう！

①約200m四方の広さに、400軒もの店が集まっています。
②場内市場が業者を対象にしているのに対して、場外市場は一般客や観光客でも利用できる店が多いのが特徴です。とはいえ、場外市場もプロの魚屋や料理人が買い付けにくる店が多く、朝一から営業し、午後一に閉店になる店も多いので注意。

Sushi 寿司

Of all the various kinds of *sushi*, the first one we tend to think of would probably be *nigiri-zushi*, with its vinegared rice topped with raw fish. *Nigiri-zushi* originated during the *Edo* period as *Edomae-zushi*, which used seafood caught in Tokyo bay. It was later to become popular throughout the country.

Surprisingly enough, the origins of *sushi* can be traced back to Southeast Asia in the 4th century BC. It originated as a method of preserving fish by packing it in rice and fermenting it. The rice was then discarded.

Sushi was later to be introduced to Japan via China. Japanese people, who have loved rice greatly since those times, kept the rice and ate it together with the fish. This established *sushi* as a type of cuisine.

From around 1980, beginning with the *sushi* boom in the USA, *sushi* has spread throughout the globe, and is eaten in countries around the world as the most representative, and most delicious, of Japanese foods.

There are various points of etiquette involved in enjoying the delicious taste of *sushi*. When picking up a piece of *sushi* with chopsticks or with your fingers, do so gently so as not to damage its shape. Do not put soy sauce directly onto pieces of *sushi*; rather, brush it with a piece of pickled sliced ginger (*gari*) dipped into the soy sauce. Do not put soy sauce on conger eel or other types of *sushi* finished with a brushed-on sweet sauce. Furthermore, you should eat each piece of *sushi* in one bite, and not take the topping off the rice or break up a piece of *sushi*.

There are many famous *sushi* restaurants in Tokyo, especially in

旅のポイント

Ginza. Sampling the *sushi* making skills of one of these long-established restaurants is one way to experience an aspect of Tokyo's food culture.

　さまざまな種類がある寿司の中で、真っ先に思い浮かべるのは酢飯（シャリ）の上に具材（ネタ）がのったにぎり寿司ではないでしょうか。にぎり寿司は、東京湾でとれる魚介を使った江戸前寿司として江戸時代に誕生し、その後全国に広がっていきました。

　しかし、意外にも寿司の起源は紀元前4世紀頃の東南アジアにさかのぼります。米の中に魚を漬けて発酵させるという魚肉保存法として誕生し、米は捨てられていました。

　その後中国大陸を経て日本に伝来。当時から米を愛してやまない日本人は、米を捨てず魚と一緒に食べるということで、寿司を料理として確立させていきました。

　1980（昭和55）年頃のアメリカのスシブームをきっかけに、全世界に広がっていった寿司は、日本の最も代表的でおいしい料理として世界中の国で食されています。

　寿司をおいしく味わうために、さまざまなマナーがあります。箸や手でとりあげる際は、形が崩れないようにそっと持ち上げること。醤油は握りを直接つけるのではなく、醤油で浸したガリで塗るようにすること。アナゴなど甘いツメを塗った寿司は醤油をつけないこと。寿司だねをはがしたり、寿司をちぎったりせずひと口で食べることなど。

　東京には銀座をはじめ、数多くの寿司の名店があります。それら老舗の技を味わうことも、東京の食文化に触れる一端といえるでしょう。

14 AREA GUIDE
Shimbashi

①There are many casual bars near the *Karasumori*
entrance on the west side of JR *Shimbashi* Station. It is
known as an office worker's district that bustles with
people on their way home from work.

②That *Karasumori* entrance area, having developed in the
late *Edo* period, was especially prosperous as a *geisha* district during the *Meiji* and *Taishō* periods, and was referred
to as the top social meeting place in Japan. That history
continues to this day as the *Shimbashi Karyūkai*, 'the
flower and willow world' of the *geisha*.

③Also, in 1872, the first railroad in Japan began operations
between *Shimbashi* and *Yokohama*, and thus *Shimbashi* is
the birthplace of Japanese railroads.

④The *Shimbashi* Station of that time is now in the

Shiodome area, and at that location a replica of the outer view of the station building(駅舎) and one part of the station platform(ホーム) are open to the public(公開される) as the Old *Shimbashi* Station. Inside the building is the Railroad History Exhibition Room. Admission is free.(入場無料)

---

14. 新橋(しんばし)
エリアガイド

①JR新橋駅西側の烏森口(からすもり)には庶民的な居酒屋が多く、会社帰りの人々で賑わう「サラリーマンの街」として知られています。

②その烏森口は、江戸時代末期に興って以来、とりわけ明治・大正時代には日本一の社交場と呼ばれるほどの花街として栄え、その歴史は「新橋花柳界(しんばしかりゅうかい)」として現代に続いています。

③また、1872（明治5）年には、新橋〜横浜間に日本初の鉄道が開業し、新橋は日本の鉄道発祥の地にもなっています。

④当時の新橋駅は現在の汐留エリアにあり、その場所は現在、駅舎外観とホームの一部を再現した「旧新橋停車場(きゅうしんばしていしゃば)」として公開されています。建物内には入場無料の鉄道歴史展示室(てつどうれきしてんじしつ)があります。

Izakaya (Japanese-style bars) 居酒屋(いざかや)

Izakaya provide food and alcoholic drinks in an informal setting at an inexpensive price. There are various theories on the definition of an *izakaya*, but the term generally refers to popular restaurants that serve alcoholic drinks, mainly Japanese sake and Japanese food. They are also called *taishū sakaba* ('popular drinking place') or *aka chōchin* (literally: 'red lantern').

The first drink ordered at an *izakaya* is typically beer. This has permeated society so much that the phrase "*toriaezu bīru*" ("I'll start with a beer.") has taken hold as a commonplace.

Izakaya serve something called *otōshi* which will be brought to you even though you have not ordered it. This is a little something served to tide you over for the short time until the first food you ordered comes to you, but it isn't free; there is a charge for it. Some establishments treat this as a kind of cover charge.

Also, the standard drink snack that you can find on the menu at almost any *izakaya* is *edamame* (soybeans in the pod). People ordering assorted *oshinko* (pickles) or *ochazuke* (rice with tea poured on it) to finish up the night is a something you will often see at an *izakaya*.

There are many *izakaya* in *Shimbashi*, *Yūrakuchō*, *Shinjuku*, *Kanda* and *Ueno*. These fill with a lively bustle of white collar workers after work. Type of *Izakaya* include *gā-do shita* bars and restaurants under the girders and arches of railway bridges and elevated tracks, and densely-packed rows of narrow back street bars and restaurants in *yokochō* side alleys. Places like this fill up completely as the sun goes down. The scene here every night is one of people moving over to make room for one another, filling the sake cups and sharing

旅のポイント

some drinks together. They engage in lively talk about work with senior and junior colleagues. They let themselves go a little, talking loudly and singing. *Izakaya* are places of recreation and relaxation, indispensable for the workers of Japan.

　手軽にかつ安い値段で、酒と料理を提供する店のことです。定義は諸説ありますが、日本酒を中心としたアルコール飲料、和食中心の料理を出す大衆的な飲食店のことを指し、大衆酒場や赤ちょうちんなどと呼ばれることもあります。

　居酒屋で最初に注文する飲み物といえば、やはりビールです。「とりあえずビール」という言葉が定着するほど浸透しています。

　そして、注文をしていないのに出されるお通しがあります。これは、最初の料理が出てくるまでの間を持たせるちょっとした料理として出されるのですが、サービスではなく有料です。これを席料として考えて提供している店もあります。

　また、どの居酒屋でも大体ある酒のつまみの定番メニューは枝豆。最後の締めにお新香盛り合わせやお茶漬けを注文するのも、居酒屋でよく見られる光景です。

　居酒屋は新橋や有楽町、新宿、神田、上野などに多く、仕事を終えたサラリーマンたちで大変なにぎわいを見せています。鉄道の高架下や周辺にある「ガード下」の店、小さな路地を入ったところに間口の狭い店が密集する「横丁」の店。夕暮れとともに満席となったそれらの店で、肩寄せあうように盃を酌み交わす風景が、毎晩のように見られます。仕事の話で上司や部下と盛り上がり、ちょっと羽目を外して大声で笑い歌い。居酒屋は日本人の働く人たちにとって、なくてはならない憩いの場でもあるのです。

15 AREA GUIDE

Nihombashi

①During the *Edo* period, this was the starting point for the five highways that ran from *Edo*. It was a district that thrived both as a center of commerce and as a fish market.
②The *Nihombashi* Bridge that gives this district its name was built on the orders of *Tokugawa Ieyasu* in 1603. The current bridge was built in 1911, and has been designated as an Important Cultural Property of Japan.
③Facilities such as the headquarters of the central bank of Japan, Bank of Japan, as well as the largest financial exchange in Japan, the Tokyo Stock Exchange, are located here, making it a leading financial district representative of Japan.

④The Bank of Japan building is a beautiful stone building designed by the famous architect *Tatsuno Kingo*, who also designed buildings such as Tokyo Station and *Ōsaka Central Public Hall*. There are many historical buildings such as this in this area, making impressive architecture another characteristic of *Nihombashi*.

大阪市中央公会堂
歴史的建築物

15. 日本橋(にほんばし)
エリアガイド

①江戸時代に五街道の起点となり、商業の中心地として、また魚河岸で賑わった街です。
②街の名にもなっている「日本橋」は、1603（慶長8）年に徳川家康(とくがわいえやす)の命で架けられました。現在の橋は1911（明治44）年の架橋で、国の重要文化財に指定されています。
③日本の中央銀行である日本銀行(にほんぎんこう)の本店や、日本最大の金融商品取引所・東京証券取引所(とうきょうしょうけんとりひきじょ)などがある、日本を代表する金融街でもあります。
④また、日本銀行は、東京駅や大阪市中央公会堂などを造った名建築家・辰野金吾(たつのきんご)の設計による美しい石造りの建物で、こういった歴史的建造物が多いのも日本橋の特徴です。

16 *Nihombashi Takashimaya*
Its trademark is the rose design on its paper bags

①*Nihombashi Takashimaya* is a long-established [老舗] department store and is among the best in Japan. It was founded [創業された] in *Kyōto* in 1831. The *Nihombashi* branch [日本橋店] opened in 1933, and its being fully furnished with [全館~を備える] the then [当時の] rare luxury of air conditioning [冷暖房装置] spread the *Takashimaya* name throughout the country.

②The *Nihombashi* branch is the first department store in Japan to be designated as [~として指定される] an Important Cultural Property [重要文化財], so be sure to take note of [~に注目する] both its interior and exterior, which maintain the style of the time of its first opening.

---

16. 日本橋髙島屋
目印はバラの花柄の紙袋

①日本を代表する老舗の百貨店です。創業地は京都で、1831（天保2）年開店。日本橋店は1933（昭和8）年に開店、当時珍しい全館冷暖房装置を備え、髙島屋の名を日本全国に広めました。

②日本橋店は百貨店建築としては初めて国の重要文化財に指定され、当時の姿を保っている内外装ともに注目です。

17 *Taimeiken*
Three generations of serving western cuisine for Japanese tastes

①Founded in 1931, this long-running [老舗] Western cuisine [洋食店] restaurant has kept the same flavor [味] established by founder [創業者] *Modegi Shingo*.

②The omelet rice [オムライス], which uses three super-high grade [特級] eggs for the omelet to wrap around [〜を包む] the ketchup-seasoned fried rice, is a signature dish [看板メニュー] of the store which has been on the menu since the restaurant was founded.

③Also, *Oryōri* 110, the free phone consultation service [電話相談] questions related to cooking continues to this day.

---

17. たいめいけん
三代にわたって作り上げてきた日本人好みの洋食

①1931（昭和6）年創業、初代・茂出木心護氏からの味を守り続ける老舗洋食店です。
②特級卵を3個も使うオムレツでケチャップライスを包んだオムライスは、創業当時から続く店の看板メニュー。
③また、料理に関する無料電話相談「お料理110番」も、現在まで続いています。

18 AREA GUIDE

Marunouchi

①*Marunouchi* is a term for the whole area on the west side of Tokyo Station. High-rise buildings such as the *Maru* building, run throughout the area. Proceed westward through this building district and the Imperial Palace will come into view directly in front of you.

②In 1890, one of Japan's three largest *zaibatsu* (financial conglomerates), *Mitsubishi Zaibatsu*, purchased the land in this area and developed *Marunouchi* as an office district. Even now, the main offices of the *Mitsubishi* Group are concentrated here in one of the main centers of Japanese business.

③The central tourist spot here is, in fact, the Tokyo Station *Marunouchi* Station building itself. The red brick building has been restored to its appearance at the time of its first opening in 1914 after almost 5 years of construction. Along the *Marunouchi-nakadōri* Boulevard, many refined (洗練された) restaurants and retail stores (物販店) can be found, and this is a popular area with women. *Nihombashi* and *Ginza* are within walking distance (徒歩圏内).

18. 丸の内
エリアガイド

①東京駅の西側一帯を指し、丸ビルをはじめとする高層ビルが連なっています。このビル街を抜けて西へ行くと皇居が目の前に現れます。

②1890(明治23)年、日本の三大財閥のひとつである三菱財閥が土地を買い取り、丸の内はオフィス街として発展。現在でも三菱グループの本社が集中する、日本のビジネスの中心地のひとつです。

③観光の中心はなんといっても、約5年の工事で1914年の創建当時の姿に復元された赤レンガ造りの東京駅丸の内駅舎。丸の内仲通りには洗練された飲食店、物販店が揃い、女性に人気。日本橋や銀座も徒歩圏内です。

19 Tokyo Station, *Marunouchi* Station Building

The retro-style red brick station building is a Tokyo landmark

①The Tokyo Station *Marunouchi* Station Building, which was constructed about 100 years ago in 1914, is a beautiful red-brick building designed by the famous architect *Tatsuno Kingo*. In 2012, it was successfully restored to the way it looked when it first opened.

②Until restoration was decided upon, it is said that there were several plans to rebuild the station building as a modern high-rise building. However, persistent voices calling for the preservation of this, a historical building befitting Japan's capital Tokyo, led to it being restored.

③Passing though the JR turnstile and looking up, you will catch sight of the ceiling adorned with beautiful decorations which are a fusion of Japan and the west. On that domed ceiling, at a height of almost 30 meters, you will see reliefs of the Chinese zodiac animals and phoenixes, along with sculptures of eagles, amongst other things.

④There is also the Tokyo Station Gallery, where you can enjoy works of art along with the brick walls of the old sta-
～を鑑賞する　　　　　　　　　　　　　　　　　　旧駅舎
tion building, and the historical Tokyo Station Hotel.

19. 東京駅丸の内駅舎
赤レンガのレトロ駅舎は、東京のランドマーク

①今からおよそ100年前、1914（大正3）年に建てられた東京駅丸の内駅舎は、名建築家・辰野金吾が設計した美しい赤レンガ造りの建物です。2012（平成24）年に開業当時の姿に復元することに成功しました。

②復元工事を決定するまでには、近代的な高層ビルに建て替える計画が何度か挙がったといいます。しかし、日本の首都・東京にふさわしい歴史的建造物を残そうという根強い声が、今回の保存復元の成功につながりました。

④JRの改札を出てすぐ、上を見上げると和と洋が融合した美しい装飾の数々が施された天井が目に入ってきます。この高さ約30ｍのドーム天井には、干支や鳳凰のレリーフ、鷲の彫刻などが見られます。

④その他、芸術作品とともに旧駅舎のレンガ壁が観賞できる東京ステーションギャラリーや、歴史ある東京ステーションホテルもあります。

20 *Mitsubishi Ichigōkan* Building
Appreciate famous works of modern western art held in an excellent example of *Meiji* architecture

①This beautiful red brick western-style office building was designed by the English architect Josiah Conder in 1894.
②It was dismantled in 1968, but based on the architectural plans from the time of its construction and measured drawings from the time of its dismantlement, along with various documents and photographs, it was rebuilt in 2010 and was reborn as an art museum.
③Exhibitions focusing on late 19th century western art are held here.

---

20. 三菱一号館
明治の名建築で近代西洋美術の名品を鑑賞

①1894（明治27）年、英国人建築家ジョサイア・コンドルによって設計された、赤レンガが美しい洋風事務所建築です。
②1968（昭和43）年に解体されましたが、当時の設計図や解体時の実測図、各種文献や写真などを基に2010（平成22）年に復元され、美術館として生まれ変わりました。
③19世紀末の西洋美術を中心に、企画展を開催しています。

21　*Meiji Seimei-kan* Building
A magnificent exterior with a beautiful colonnade and column head ornamentation

①Completed in 1934, this steel reinforced concrete building
　　竣工された　　　　　　　　　　　鉄骨鉄筋コンクリート
was the first *Shōwa* period building to be designated as an

Important Cultural Property.
　　重要文化財
②This building has seen turbulent times since, at the end of
　　　　　　　　　　　激動の時代
the Pacific War, it became the venue for the representatives
　太平洋戦争　　　　　　　　　　会場
of the United States, the United Kingdom, China, and the

Soviet Union to meet as the Allied Council for Japan.
　　　　　　　　　　　　　　対日理事会

---

21. 明治生命館
重厚な外観、列柱や柱頭装飾が美しい

①1934（昭和9）年竣工で、昭和の建造物としては初めて国の重要文化財に指定された、鉄骨鉄筋コンクリート造りのビルです。
②太平洋戦争終結後には、米・英・中・ソの4か国の代表による対日理事会（ACJ）の会場となり、激動の時代を見つめてきました。

22 AREA GUIDE

The Imperial Palace

① The Imperial Palace area includes buildings such as the residence (住居) of their Majesties the Emperor and Empress (天皇皇后両陛下), the palace (宮殿) where various events are carried out, and government office buildings (庁舎) of the Imperial Household Agency (宮内庁).
② It was originally the castle of the shoguns of the *Tokugawa* shogunate (徳川幕府), and remained so (そのままであった) for a span of 270 years. With the transfer of the national capital to Tokyo (東京奠都) in 1869, however, the Emperor moved here from the Imperial Palace in *Kyōto* (京都御所), making this the new Imperial residence.
③ Currently, you can freely walk around and explore the Outer Gardens (外苑) of the Imperial Palace, with the *Nijū-bashi* (二重橋) Bridge which is sometimes often regarded as a representative feature of the Imperial Palace. Entry into the East Garden (東御苑) of the Imperial Palace, the extensive (広大な) garden that

54

richly preserves vestiges of *Edo*, is free.
　　　　　　　　　面影

④The area around the *Kita-no-Maru* Park, located to the
　　　　　　　　　　北の丸公園

north, with locations including the National Museum of
　　　　　　　　　　　　　　　　東京国立近代美術館

Modern Art, the *Nippon Budōkan*, and the Science
　　　　　　　　　　　　　　　　　　　　　　科学技術館

Museum, is also worthy of attention.

22. 皇居
エリアガイド

①皇居には天皇皇后両陛下の住居である御所をはじめ、諸行事を行う宮殿、宮内庁関係の庁舎などの建物があります。
②もとは270年にもわたった徳川幕府の将軍の居城でしたが、1869（明治2）年の東京奠都で、京都御所から天皇が移られ、皇居となりました。
③現在、皇居の顔とも呼ばれる二重橋のある皇居外苑は、自由に歩き散策することができます。また、江戸の面影を色濃く残す広大な庭園である皇居東御苑も入園無料です。
④そのほか、北側に位置する東京国立近代美術館や日本武道館、科学技術館などがある北の丸公園周辺にも注目です。

23

Hibiya Park
The first western-style park in Japan

①*Hibiya* Park opened in 1903 as a pioneer modern city park.
　　　　　　　　　　　　　　　　　　　先駆け

②The soothing spaces provided by the large fountains and
　　　癒しの　　　　　　　　　　　　　　　　噴水
flower beds, and the *Shinji-ike* Pond that extends through
花壇　　　　　　　心字池
the gardens, spreads throughout the park grounds. Also,

Hibiya Park Large Concert Hall, the first outdoor concert
日比谷公園大音楽堂
hall in Japan which is familiar to many as '*Yaon*', and the

multi-purpose hall *Hibiya* Public Hall are widely known.
多目的の　　　　　　　　日比谷公会堂

---

23. 日比谷公園
日本で最初の洋式公園

①1903（明治36）年に、近代都市公園の先駆けとして開園しました。
②園内は大噴水や大花壇、心字池が広がる庭園など癒しの空間が広がっています。ほかに「野音」として親しまれている日本初の野外音楽堂である日比谷公園大音楽堂、多目的ホールの日比谷公会堂も広く知られています。

第2章●東京中心部

24 The Diet Building
Often called the chalk palace, this is the political center of Japan

①The Diet building in *Nagata-chō*, the central area of Japanese politics. It is the place where the National Diet (国会) is held.
②Designed symmetrically (左右対称に), it is arranged with the Lower House (衆議院) on the left and the Upper House (参議院) on the right as one faces the front of the building.

③Tours of the Upper House are possible on any weekday when it is not in session (本会議開催中), and tours of the Lower House are possible if you apply for (〜を申し込む) a tour before 4 PM on the day before you wish to take the tour.

---

24. 国会議事堂
「白亜の殿堂」と称される、日本政治の中心

①日本の政治の中枢地区・永田町にある国会が開催される建物です。
②左右対称の設計になっていて、正面向かって左に衆議院、右に参議院を配しています。
③参議院は本会議開催中以外の平日ならいつでも、衆議院も見学の前日の午後4時までに申込みをすれば見学が可能です。

旅のポイント

Tokyo Souvenirs 東京みやげ

Tokyo, with its many shops and many things to buy, also offers an abundant variety of souvenirs. Standard Tokyo souvenirs are all available at locations such as *Haneda* Airport and main stations within the metropolitan area including Tokyo Station and *Shinagawa* Station.

Souvenirs differ from area to area. Standard sightseeing souvenirs from Tokyo, such as goods from Tokyo Skytree or Tokyo Tower, are popular. Souvenirs such as Japanese sweets from a long-established shop are also sure to please the recipient.

　店も物も多い東京は、おみやげの種類も豊富です。東京駅や品川駅といった都内の主要な駅や羽田空港などには、定番の東京みやげが揃っています。

　また、各エリアによっておみやげも変わります。東京スカイツリーや東京タワーのグッズなどは、東京観光の定番みやげとして人気がありますし、老舗の和菓子などもおみやげとして喜ばれるでしょう。

Chapter 3

Traditional Tokyo

....

第3章
東京下町

25 AREA GUIDE

Asakusa

①This area is typical as it preserves the charm of (魅力) the old downtown districts (下町) of Tokyo known as *Shitamachi*. With Tokyo's oldest temple the *Sensō-ji* at its center, this area features a number of unique (個性的な) streets such as the merchant street (商店街) *Nakamise* with its traditional Japanese grocery stores (雑貨店), the *objet d'art* (オブジェ) *Dembō-in* street (伝法院通り) with its *Edo*-style streets and stores, or the Hoppy street (ホッピー通り) with its relaxed, affordable (手ごろな) bars.

②The main walking route in *Asakusa* starts from *Nakamise* with the landmark *Kaminari-mon* Gate and its great paper lantern (提灯) towards the *Sensō-ji* temple. On the small side roads (路地) running lengthways and crossways along this route you will see Tokyo as it was in the good old days. This area also offers a great variety of (多彩な) restaurants and bars including restaurants with a long history of serving traditional dishes. ③If you cross the *Azuma-bashi* Bridge, a 15 minute walk (徒歩5分) will bring you to the Tokyo Skytree. The walk is an enjoyable one, with the tower soaring up (昇る) into the sky in front of you as you go (歩いていくうちに).

25. 浅草
エリアガイド

①東京を代表する下町風情が残るエリアです。東京最古の寺である浅草寺を中心に、和小物など日本テイストの雑貨が揃う商店街の仲見世、沿道や店の屋根などに江戸情緒を彷彿させるオブジェを配した伝法院通り、開放的な大衆酒場が連なるホッピー通りなど、個性的な通りがいくつも延びています。

②大きな提灯がランドマークの雷門を起点に、仲見世から浅草寺へと歩くのがメインルートですが、縦横に走っている路地も昔ながらの東京の面影を色濃く残しています。歴史ある名店など、飲食店のジャンルも多彩です。

③吾妻橋を渡れば、徒歩15分で東京スカイツリーへ。空にそびえるタワーを見上げながらの散歩も楽しいものです。

26 *Sensō-ji* temple
Asakusa landmark and Tokyo's oldest temple

①Built in the year 628, *Sensō-ji* is Tokyo's oldest temple. It has for many years (長年) been loved as the *Asakusa Kan'non-sama* (the *Asakusa* temple of Avalokiteśvara). The temple consists of (〜からなる) the *Kaminari-mon* Gate, the main hall (本堂), the five-storied pagoda (五重塔), and the *Hōzō-mon* Gate. Many of the temple's halls and other structures were destroyed by fire (焼失した) in the 1945 Great Tokyo Air Raid (東京大空襲). The temple buildings were restored (再建された) after the war, and the *Niten-mon* Gate, which escaped the conflagration (大火災), was designated as (〜として指定された) an Important Cultural Property (重要文化財).

②The *Kaminari-mon* Gate with its distinctive large paper lantern (提灯) is officially named *Fūraijin-mon*. Pass through the *Hōzō-mon* gate with its deva guardian figures (仁王像), and the main hall with its characteristic steep (急な) roof appears in front of you. The main object of worship (御本尊) is the bodhisattva Avalokiteśvara (聖観世音菩薩). At either side of the gold-layered miniature (小型の)

shrine called the *gokūden* are Brahmā (*Bon-ten*) and Śakra Devānām Indra (*Taishaku-ten*).

③The temple's seasonal ceremonies such as the *Hōzuki-ichi* held on July 9-10th and the *Hagoita-ichi* on December 17-19th attract many visitors.
　　　　　　　　行事
　開催される

26. 浅草寺（せんそうじ）

浅草のランドマークである、都内最古の寺院

①628年に創建された都内最古の寺院で、浅草の観音様として古くから親しまれてきました。雷門に本堂、五重塔、宝蔵門（ほうぞうもん）などからなり、多くの堂宇が1945（昭和20）年の東京大空襲によって焼失。戦後になってから再建されている中、災禍を逃れた二天門（にてんもん）が重要文化財に指定されています。
②大きな提灯が目印の雷門は、正式名称は風雷神門（ふうらいじんもん）といいます。仁王像を安置する宝蔵門をくぐると、急勾配の屋根が特徴の本堂が。御本尊は聖観世音菩薩（しょうかんぜおんぼさつ）で、総金箔押しの御宮殿の左右には梵天（ぼんてん）と帝釈天（たいしゃくてん）がまつられています。
③季節ごとにさまざまな行事も行われていて、7月9・10日に行われる「ほおずき市」、12月17～19日に行われる「羽子板市（はごいたいち）」は、多くのお客を集めています。

27 *Nakamise*
A very Japanese shopping area that bustles with foreigners

① This old shopping street with its 90 or so stores runs 250 meters from the *Kaminari-mon* Gate to the *Hōzō-mon* Gate of the *Sensō-ji* temple. It has origins during the years 1688-1736, when the people responsible for cleaning within the temple precincts were permitted to open stores along the approach to the temple. This grew into a bustling area around the temple gates, with souvenir, sweets and toy stores.

② The stores, adorned with red paper lanterns, mostly sell items based on traditional Japanese goods and culture. Here, many foreigners are to be seen in addition to the Japanese visitors. Visitors will find stores selling Japanese art and craft items such as hair accessories, Japanese umbrellas, folding fans and Japanese-style wooden clogs. Some stores also offer nostalgic Japanese snacks and confectionery such as *mitarashi dango* dumplings, hand fried *sembei* rice crackers, and deep fried *manjū* (yeast cakes filled with bean paste) sweets.

③Also popular is *ningyō yaki kasutera* cake, a famous product of the downtown areas of Tokyo. These five-storied pagoda or lantern-shaped cakes contain sweet bean paste inside it.

---

27. 仲見世
外国人で賑わう日本情緒の商店街

①雷門から浅草寺の宝蔵門まで、250mほどの参道に90軒ほどの店舗が並ぶ商店街です。元禄〜享保年間（1688〜1736）、浅草寺境内の清掃役だった人たちに参道への出店を許可したことが起源で、みやげものや菓子、おもちゃを扱う店が並ぶ門前町として、賑わいを見せたのが始まりです。
②店頭に赤い提灯が掛けられた店舗のほとんどが、日本の伝統にのっとった品を扱っており、日本人のみならず多くの外国人観光客の姿も見られます。かんざし、和傘、扇子、下駄といった和雑貨をはじめ、みたらし団子、手焼きせんべい、揚げ饅頭といった、懐かしい味わいの和菓子も。
③五重塔や提灯をモチーフにしたカステラ生地にあんを包んだ、下町名物のお菓子「人形焼き」も人気の品です。

28

Asakusa Hanayashiki
A retro entertainment park full of thrills

①This underline{entertainment park} opened in 1853, and is Japan's
　　　　　　　　遊園地
oldest. It retains a retro *Shōwa* period atmosphere even
　　　　～を保つ　　　　　　昭和
today.

②Built in 1953, the roller coaster has been a popular attrac-
　　　　　　　　　　　　　　　　　　　　　　　　　　　　アトラクション
tion for over 60 years. With a top speed of 42kph it is rather
　60年以上　　　　　　　　　　　　　　　　時速～km
slow. In addition, the park offers many attrac-

tions for children to enjoy, such as the merry-

go-round and a 6-meter high big wheel.
　　　　　　　　　～メートルの高さの

28. 浅草花やしき
スリル満点のレトロ遊園地

①開園は1853（嘉永6）年の日本最古の遊園地で、昭和の頃のレトロな雰囲気を今もなお伝えています。
②ローラーコースターは1953（昭和28）年に設置されたもので、60年以上も運行する人気のアトラクションです。最高時速は42kmとゆっくりで、ほかメリーゴーラウンドや高さ6mの観覧車など、子どもが楽しめるアトラクションが豊富です。

29 The *Asakusa Engei* Hall
A temple of *Shitamachi* performing arts

①The *Asakusa Engei* Hall is a theater for regular performances of *rakugo* (Japanese traditional comic storytelling) which opened in 1964. The *Engei* Hall is *Asakusa*'s only *rakugo* stage. Here, you can enjoy a wide range of entertainment including *rakugo*, *manzai* and *mandan* comedy acts.

②The *Asakusa Engei* Hall is open every day of the year, and audiences are never turned out during a day's performances. This, then, is a place where you can enjoy *rakugo* whenever you wish and for as long as you like.

---

29. 浅草演芸ホール
下町芸能の殿堂

①1964（昭和39）年に開場した、落語の定席です。浅草における唯一の落語寄席で、落語をはじめ漫才に漫談など、多彩な演芸を鑑賞できます。

②年中無休で入替なしのため、好きな時に好きなだけ落語を楽しめます。

30. Old shops in *Asakusa*: The *Kamiya* Bar
The birthplace of *denki buran*

① This long-established bar has been a bustling social spot in *Shitamachi* since it opened in 1880.

② The bar's signature cocktail is the *denki buran*, a brandy base drink with gin, wine, curacao and other elements mixed in the traditional secret proportions.

③ The origin of the drink's name goes back to the *Meiji* period when electricity (*denki*) was still rare and the word *denki* was attached to anything new.

---

30. 浅草の老舗：神谷バー
デンキブラン発祥の酒場

① 1880（明治13）年の創業以来、下町の社交場として賑わってきた老舗バーです。
② 店の看板であるカクテルのデンキブランは、ブランデーをベースにジン、ワイン、キュラソーなどを、秘伝の分量で加えたものです。
③ 名の由来はまだ電気が珍しい明治期に、新しいものに「電気○○」とつけたことによります。

31 Old shops in *Asakusa* : *Yagembori*

A specialist store dedicated to *shichimi* spices

①Established in 1625, this is one of *Asakusa*'s oldest shops. It has been in business (営業している) for over 380 years, specializing exclusively in (〜のみを) *shichimi*, a blend of seven spices.
②*Shichimi* is a condiment (調味料) consisting (〜からなる) of a mix of cayenne pepper, *chimpi* (a type of dried orange peel (ミカンの皮)), black sesame, poppy seeds (ケシの実), the Japanese pepper known as *sanshō*, and linseed (麻の実). Here, one can buy *shichimi* made up according to (〜に合わせて) one's taste (好み) in spiciness (辛さ) and fragrance (香り).

31. 浅草の老舗：やげん堀
この道一筋の七味専門店

①1625（寛永2）年創業の浅草で屈指の老舗で、380年以上もの間、七味ひと筋で商売を続けている専門店です。
②七味とは、生唐辛子に焼き唐辛子、陳皮、黒ゴマ、ケシの実、粉サンショウ、麻の実を混ぜた調味料です。辛さと香りを、好みに合わせて調合してもらうこともできます。

32 The *Kappa-bashi* utensils street
Every conceivable cooking utensil can be found here

①This 800 meter long shopping street is located precisely between *Asakusa* and *Ueno*. With over 170 kitchen equipment and tableware stores, it offers anything and everything needed in the professional catering industry.

②Stores here offer everything from kitchen equipment and utensils to commercial foodstuffs, tableware and wrapping materials. There is also plenty here to interest the general customer, with stores specializing in crockery, confectionary making equipment, and home-kitchen utensils. These can all be obtained for less than market prices.

③The Japanese kitchen knives and plastic food samples available in this area are popular among foreigners. The samples are intricately worked to be almost identical to the original *sushi*, side dishes or sweets they represent. Model versions of these plastic samples, and key or phone straps featuring them are popular as souvenirs.

④The *Kappa-bashi* festival is held every year in October. At
　　かっぱ橋道具まつり
this time, a memorial ceremony called the *dōgu kuyōsai* is

performed in appreciation of the cooking utensils that after
　　　　　～に感情をこめて
many years of use have come to the end of their lives.
　　　　　　　　　　　　　寿命を迎えた

32. かっぱ橋道具街
料理用具で手に入らないものはない

①浅草と上野のちょうど中間に位置する、約800mにわたる商店街です。調理用具や食器などの店が170ほど並ぶ、飲食業のプロの御用達の街です。

②扱っている品々は、厨房設備や器具、業務用食材のほか、各種食器類や包装用品など、一般客にも興味がわきそうなものも。陶器の専門店や製菓用品、家庭向き台所用品もあり、市価より安く手に入ります。

③外国人に人気なのが、和包丁や食品サンプル。寿司や惣菜、スイーツのサンプルは本物と見間違うほど精密な仕上がりで、オブジェやストラップなどのおみやげにも人気です。

④毎年10月中旬には「かっぱ橋道具まつり」が開催され、長年使用した料理道具に感謝を込めての「道具供養祭」も行われます。

旅のポイント

The taste of *Shitamachi*: loach cuisine
下町伝統の味・どぜう料理

Loach cuisine makes an affordable and filling meal, as good as eel in terms of nourishment, that has long been popular among the people of *Edo*. Around the *Asakusa* area there are many establishments serving this cuisine that were founded in the *Edo* and *Meiji* periods. They compete to define the authentic taste of this dish. Loach cuisine is typically prepared and served in a pot known as a *nabe*. The loach is pacified with sake then boiled in *warishita* (a seasoning made from soy sauce, stock and *mirin*, a sweetened sake), chopped spring onions and *shichimi* spices amongst other things.

The taste and kinds of loaches cooked differ from restaurant to restaurant. The *Dojō Iidaya* restaurant is known for its obsession with the quality of its carefully selected native loaches.

　ウナギに負けず劣らずの栄養、しかも値段が手ごろで、古くから江戸庶民のスタミナ料理として味わわれてきたどぜう（ドジョウ）料理。浅草界隈には江戸や明治創業の老舗が点在しており、伝統の味を競っています。

　ドジョウの料理法は鍋が中心で、酒に酔わせて静かにさせたドジョウを割下で煮込み、ネギをたっぷりのせて七味などを振ってからいただきます。

　味付けや使うドジョウは、店ごとにさまざまな流儀があります。「どぜう飯田屋」では、厳選した天然もののドジョウにこだわっています。

旅のポイント

The taste of *Edo*-style *soba*
江戸の老舗のそばを味わう

Yabu, like *Sarashina* and *Sunaba*, is the name for one grouping of Tokyo's long established *soba* buckwheat noodle restaurants. The name *Yabu* has been in use since the *Edo* period. Its origin is, as the name suggests, the familiar name given to a restaurant that stands among bushes (*yabu*). As the *soba* buckwheat noodles served by this restaurant were so delicious, the term *yabu* spread as a name for good *soba* restaurants.

The original *yabu soba* restaurant is the *Kanda-yabu-soba* in the *Kanda* area. Together with the *Namiki-yabu-soba* and *Ike-no-hata-yabu-soba* they are known as the big three of *yabu soba* or *yabu gosanke*. The thick and salty taste of the sauce dip for the *soba* is a characteristic feature. This taste comes from the habit of native Tokyoites, who enjoy their *soba* only with only the slightest dip of sauce.

「更科」、「砂場」と並ぶ、東京のそばの老舗である「藪」。江戸時代から使われていた屋号で、起源は文字通り藪の中にあった店の愛称だったといわれています。その店のそばがおいしかったことから、うまいそば屋を表す屋号として広まっていったとされます。

藪蕎麦の本家は神田にある「かんだやぶそば」で、ここと「並木藪蕎麦」、「池之端藪蕎麦」が「藪御三家」と称されています。そばつゆの味が濃く塩辛いのが特徴で、つゆをちょっとだけつけて食べる江戸っ子の流儀はこの影響です。

33 Tokyo Skytree®
A view over *Shitamachi* and the center of Tokyo

① The Skytree® is Tokyo's number one tourist spot. At 634 meters, it is the world's highest free-standing steel radio tower. The Tokyo Skytree Town® consists of Tokyo *Solamachi*'s 300 restaurants and shops, and tourist facilities such as the *Sumida* Aquarium and the Konica Minolta *Tenkū* planetarium.

② From the Skytree observatory you can see out across the entire center of Tokyo. Immediately below you is the *Sumida-gawa* River and *Asakusa*, a little further away you can see the Imperial Palace and the skyscrapers of *Shinjuku*. On clear days you will be able to see Mt. *Fuji*. At the *Tembō* Deck observatory you can enjoy the view while eating at the Sky Restaurant 634 (*Musashi*) or shop at the Skytree Shop, which sells official Skytree goods.

③ The tube-shaped observatory '*Tembō Galleria*' is a glass

corridor installed at a height of 445 meters. You can climb
　　回廊

this sloping corridor up to Floor 450 at

a height of 451.21 meters where the

glass walls and LED lights on the floor

help you experience the expanse of sky
　　　　　　　　　　　　　　空の広がり
before you and a feeling of floating.
　　　　　　　　　　浮遊感

33. 東京スカイツリー®
とうきょう

東京の都心・下町を眼下に一望

---

①東京でナンバーワンの観光スポットで、自立式の鉄塔としては世界一の高さとなる634mの電波塔を中心に、300店の飲食物販施設が集まる東京ソラマチ、すみだ水族館、コニカミノルタプラネタリウム"天空"などの観光施設が集まった、東京スカイツリータウン®が形成されています。
　　　　　　　　　　　てんくう

②展望台からは東京の都心を一望でき、眼下には隅田川や浅草、遠くには皇居や新宿の高層ビル群が、天気がいい日には富士山まで遠望できます。地上350mにある展望台「天望デッキ」には、食事をしながら景色を楽しめる「スカイレストラン634（むさし）」、オフィシャルグッズを扱う「ザ・スカイツリー・ショップ」があります。

③さらに上の地上445mには、チューブ状に張り出したガラスの回廊「天望回廊」が設けられています。このスロープを上がった451.21mの「フロア450」では、ガラスの壁と床面のLEDで大空の広がりや浮遊感を演出しています。

A trip through *Shitamachi* by water bus
水上バスで下町さんぽ

The *Shitamachi* downtown area lies between the *Arakawa* and *Sumida-gawa* Rivers. You can travel on these Rivers and in Tokyo bay using one of the many water buses available.

Tokyo's most popular water route is the *Sumida-gawa* line operated by the Tokyo Cruise Ship Co. Ltd. It offers a 40 minute cruise between *Asakusa* and the *Hinode-sambashi* Pier. The tour departs from the *Azuma-bashi* Bridge in *Asakusa* and continues through *Komagata-bashi* Bridge, *Umaya-bashi* Bridge, *Kuramae-bashi* Bridge, *Kiyosu-bashi* Bridge, *Eitai-bashi* Bridge, and the *Kachidoki-bashi* Bridge, known as the biggest moveable bridge in Asia. In total, the cruise passes 12 bridges of different designs and colors as it makes its way down the river. From the *Hinode-sambashi* Pier you will have a view of the Rainbow Bridge.

Other courses generally pass through Tokyo bay. There is a direct route from *Asakusa* to *Odaiba*, a route from *Hinode-sambashi* Pier to Palette Town and to Tokyo Big Sight. Futuristically designed water buses '*Hotaruna*' and '*Himiko*' designed by science fiction manga comic book author *Reiji Matsumoto* are very popular.

The Tokyo *Mizube* Line also offers cruises along the *Sumida-gawa* River. This route goes past the *Hama-rikyū* (Imperial Villa) and passes under the Rainbow Bridge. It comes to an end at the *Odabai Kaihin* Park. From the Sea Park course connecting the *Odaiba Kaihin* Park and the *Kasai Rinkai* Park you can see the Tokyo Gate Bridge known as 'the new entranceway to Tokyo bay'. In addition, there are also routes connecting to the *Kanda-gawa* River and *Nihon-bashi* or *Ryōgoku*. The small '*Kawasemi*' water bus is convenient as

旅のポイント

it offers various routes and landing points, and the departures are regular and frequent.

　荒川と隅田川の、2本の河川が縦断する下町。それらの河川や東京湾をめぐり、水上バスの航路が多数設けられています。

　一番人気の東京都観光汽船の隅田川ラインは、浅草と日の出桟橋を結ぶ所要約40分のクルーズです。浅草の吾妻橋のたもとを出発して、駒形橋や厩橋、蔵前橋、清洲橋や永代橋、さらに「東洋一の可動橋」と呼ばれた勝鬨橋など、造りや塗装が様々な十二の橋を眺めながらくぐり、川を下っていきます。日の出桟橋からはレインボーブリッジも一望できます。

　ほか浅草からお台場へ直通する航路、日の出桟橋からパレットタウンや東京ビッグサイトを結ぶ航路など、主に湾内の航路を運航しています。SF漫画家の松本零士がデザインした、近未来的な外観の水上バス「ホタルナ」「ヒミコ」が評判です。

　東京湾水辺公社も隅田川を下る水上バスを運行しており、浜離宮を経てレインボーブリッジの下をくぐり、お台場海浜公園まで至ります。また、お台場海浜公園と葛西臨海公園を結ぶシーパークコースからは、新しい東京湾の玄関となった東京ゲートブリッジを一望。ほかにも神田川や日本橋、両国などを結ぶコースも運行しています。小型の水上バス「カワセミ」が、様々な水路や船着き場へフットワーク良く運航しています。

34 AREA GUIDE

Ryōgoku

①This area centers on the *Ryōgoku Kokugikan*, which hosts tournaments of Japan's national 'sport', *sumō* wrestling.
本場所　　　　　　　　　　　　国技　　　　　　　大相撲

This is a real *sumō* town, where many *sumō* stables
相撲部屋
are to be found. If you walk through this area you will encounter *sumō* wrestlers up close, with their traditional
〜に出くわす　　力士　　　　間近に
chommage hairstyle and *yukata* dress. This area also offers many places and stores related *sumō* other than the *Kokugikan* which are well worth a visit.
〜の価値がある

②Along *Kokugikan-dōri* which leads away from the west
西口
exit of *Ryōgoku* Station, you will see images of *sumō* wrestlers entering the ring along the road. In this area you will
土俵入りする
also find many restaurants serving the traditional *sumō* wrestler dish known as *chanko nabe*, as well as stores sell-
料理
ing oversized clothing.
ビッグサイズの

③Near this area you can also visit the remains of *Kira Kōzukenosuke*'s mansion which was raided by the *Akōroshi* (better known in English as the forty seven *rōnin*). You also can visit other *Edo* period historical sites such as the *Ekō-in* temple where you may find the grave of *Nezumi Kozō Jirokichi*, an *Edo* period Robin Hood.

34. 両国
エリアガイド

①日本の国技である大相撲が開催される両国国技館を中心に、力士が所属する相撲部屋が点在する、まさに相撲の街です。街を歩いているとちょんまげに浴衣姿の力士の姿を間近に見られ、ゆかりの見どころや店も随所に点在しています。

②両国駅の西口から延びる国技館通りには、沿道に力士の土俵入りの像が並んでいます。力士たちの食事であるちゃんこ鍋の店や、ビッグサイズの衣類を扱う洋品店などもあり、訪ね歩くのも楽しいです。

③周辺には赤穂浪士が討ち入りをした吉良上野介の上屋敷跡、江戸期の義賊である鼠小僧次郎吉の墓がある回向院など、江戸時代からの史跡も見どころです。

35 — Ryōgoku Kokugikan
Three *sumō* tournaments are held here every year

①Built in 1984 for the Japan *Sumō* Association (日本相撲協会), the *Kokugikan* holds three tournaments (本場所) per year in January, May and September. Inside the *Kokugikan* you will find colorful banners bearing the names of (〜の名前を冠した) *sumō* wrestlers (力士).

②The building can hold (〜を収容する) 11098 visitors. On the first floor are the *tamari seki* seats right next to (〜のすぐ隣に) the *sumō* ring (土俵), and the *masu seki* seating area where 4-6 people per compartment (区画) can watch the bouts (一番) while sitting on *zabuton* cushions. The second floor offers regular seats from which to enjoy watching the bouts.

③At the gift shops (売店) inside the hall you can find the printed ranking tables (番付表) known as *banzukehyō*, wrestler's handprints (手形) on colored paper and *sumō* wrestler goods such as *manjū* cakes in the shape of *sumō* wrestlers. The *yakitori* grilled chicken (焼き鳥) made inside the *Kokugikan* is excellent, and a delicious and popular accompaniment (〜のおとも) to the *sumō* bouts.

80

④The *Sumō* Museum inside the *Kokugikan* exhibits the
　　相撲博物館　　　　　　　　　　　　　　　　　　～を展示する

decorative aprons worn by *sumō* wrestlers, handprints of
　　化粧まわし

the wrestlers, old ranking tables, colored wood prints, pic-
　　　　　　　　　　　　　　　　　　　　錦絵

tures and other materials relating

to the history of *sumō*.

35. 両国国技館
大相撲本場所が年3回開かれる

①1984（昭和59）年に完成した日本相撲協会の拠点で、国技である大相撲の本場所が1月・5月・9月の年3回開催されます。場所中は力士の名前が染め抜かれた色とりどりの幟（のぼり）が、賑わいを見せています。

②建物の収容人員は1万1098名で、1階には臨場感あふれる土俵際の「溜席（たまりせき）」と、ひと区画あたり定員4～6名の座布団に座って観戦する座敷席「マス席」が設けられています。2階は椅子席で、土俵を見下ろして観戦が楽しめます。

③館内の売店では番付表や手形入りの色紙、力士の形をした「角力（すもう）まんじゅう」をはじめとした力士グッズも販売されています。国技館内で焼いている焼き鳥も、味の良さで観戦のおともに人気の逸品です。

④館内の相撲博物館には、歴代横綱の化粧まわしや手形、番付表、錦絵や写真など、相撲の歴史にまつわる資料が展示されています。

36 The *Edo*-Tokyo Museum
Learning the history of old *Edo* and modern Tokyo

①This museum introduces the history and culture of *Edo* and Tokyo from the beginning of the *Edo* shogunate (江戸幕府), through the *Meiji* and *Taishō* periods (明治・大正時代) to the Tokyo Olympic Games (東京オリンピック) in the postwar *Shōwa* period (昭和). The key feature of this museum is its easy-to-understand (分かりやすい) displays consisting of (〜からなる) original-size (実物大の) models (模型) and dioramas. The museum holds (〜を収蔵する) over 2500 historical items including 50 reconstruction (復元) models.

②Inside the museum, near the entrance you will see a reconstructed model of half the length of the *Nihom-bashi* Bridge. Passing the bridge you will find a 30:1 scale (30分の1スケール) model of a *Kan'ei*-period (寛永) (1624–1644) merchant town (町人地). The exhibition (展示) continues with models of old *Edo* terrace houses (長屋) and an actual-size model of the *Nakamuraza* playhouse (芝居小屋).

③Entering the Tokyo exhibition, you will find models of the Nicholai-*dō* church and the *Rokumeikan* (originally a guest house (迎賓館) and banqueting hall (宴会場) where foreign dignitaries were

entertained), illustrating Japan's modernization. Other
文明開化
items include terrace houses of the *Shitamachi* downtown area and models of houses illustrating life during the *Shōwa* period. The exhibition continues with displays on the history of the Great Tokyo Air Raid and the city's postwar
東京大空襲 　　　　　　　　　　　　　　　　戦後
reconstruction.
復興

36. 江戸東京博物館 (えどとうきょうはくぶつかん)
江戸から東京への時代の移り変わりを学ぶ

① 江戸幕府の開府に始まり、明治・大正・戦後昭和の東京オリンピックまでの期間を中心とした、江戸・東京の歴史や文化を紹介する博物館です。実物大の模型やジオラマなどを用いた分かりやすい展示が特徴で、復元模型50点をはじめ2500点に及ぶ資料を収蔵しています。

② 入口を入ると、半分の長さを復元した日本橋の模型が目を引きます。ここを渡ると江戸の展示で、30分の1のスケールでつくられた寛永(かんえい)の町人地、江戸庶民が生活していた長屋や芝居小屋中村座の原寸大模型など、江戸時代の町のたたずまいが伝わってくる展示が続きます。

③ 東京の展示に入ると、文明開化期の雰囲気を伝えるニコライ堂や鹿鳴館(ろくめいかん)といった洋館の模型、下町の長屋や昭和の住宅の実物大模型などが。さらに東京大空襲、戦後復興にまつわる展示と続きます。

37 AREA GUIDE

Ueno

①The area around *Ueno* Station is famous for the *Ueno Onshi* Park (上野恩賜公園) which hosts Japan's leading museums and art galleries (美術館), as well the *Ueno* Zoo with its lovable (愛らしい) pandas, and the lively (活気ある) shopping area *Ameya Yokochō*.

②The starting point for a walk through this area is *Ueno* Station. From here you can tour (～を見て回る) the galleries in the *Ueno Onshi* Park before enjoying the fresh food (生鮮品), confectionary (菓子類) and fashion stores in *Ameya Yokochō*.

③The *Shinobazu-no-ike* Pond (不忍池) on the west side of the *Ueno Onshi* Park is a natural pond of about 2 kilometers in circumference (周囲); at its center you will find the *Shinobazu-benten-dō* Buddhist prayer hall (お堂).

④If you are looking for a place to eat, you should go over to *Ueno-hirokōji* on south side of the park. Here you will find

<u>long-established</u> stores serving traditional <u>dishes</u> such as
老舗　　　　　　　　　　　　　　　　　　　料理
tonkatsu (deep-fried pork cutlet), eel or *oden* (a seasonal
soup with various <u>ingredients</u> such as *kon'nyaku*, <u>pro-</u>
　　　　　　　　　　具
<u>cessed fish</u>, eggs and vegetables).
魚の加工食品（ちくわなど）

37. 上野
エリアガイド

①日本を代表する名だたる美術館や博物館が集中する上野恩賜公園を中心に、愛らしいパンダのいる上野動物園、活気あふれる商店街のアメヤ横丁などが、上野駅周辺に集まっています。
②散策の起点は上野駅で、上野恩賜公園の美術館巡りや、アメヤ横丁での生鮮品やお菓子やファッション関連のショッピングが、主なポイントとなります。
③上野恩賜公園の西寄りにある不忍池は、周囲2kmほどの天然の池で、中央には八角形の不忍弁天堂があります。
④食事をするなら、公園の南側の上野広小路へ。とんかつやうなぎ、おでんなど伝統の老舗が点在しています。

38 *Ueno Onshi* Park

Japan's first public park, and one of Tokyo's finest spots for cherry blossom viewing

①*Ueno Onshi* Park was established in 1873 as Japan's first officially designated public park. The park stretches for over 530000 square meters on the west side of *Ueno* Station. Initially, the park was within the precincts of the *Kan'ei-ji*, a temple established by the third shogun of the *Edo* shogunate *Tokugawa Iemitsu*. The temple buildings and the *Ueno Tōshō-gū* shrine were originally the center of the park. A zoo and various museums and art galleries were later built, making the park a center for culture and the arts in Tokyo.

②Over 1200 cherry trees stand in the park. It has been a popular spot for cherry blossom viewing since the *Edo* period. Many people visit the park in early April to enjoy the cherry blossoms either by day or lit up at night.

③You will find various monuments and places of historic interest in the park. These include the bronze statue of

Saigō Takamori in memory of the bloodless surrender of
無血開城
Edo castle and the *Ueno Tōshō-gū* shrine with its 3600
江戸城
peony flowers.
ぼたん

38. 上野恩賜公園
うえ の おん し こうえん

日本初の公園は、東京屈指のサクラの名所

①1873(明治6)年に日本で初めて公園に指定された、上野駅の西側に広がる53万㎡の公園です。もとは江戸幕府3代将軍・徳川家光が建立した寛永寺の境内で、その堂宇や上野東照宮を中心とした公園だったのが、後に動物園や美術館、博物館がつくられ、現在では東京の文化や芸術の拠点となっています。

②園内には1200本ものサクラが植えられ、江戸時代から花見の名所でした。4月上旬には多くの花見客で賑わいを見せ、ライトアップされた夜桜も楽しめます。

③ほかにも、江戸城無血開城の報恩で建てられた西郷隆盛の銅像、3600株が植えられたぼたん園がある上野東照宮などの、モニュメントや史跡も見どころです。

39 *Ueno* Zoo
Let's go and see the pandas!

①Ueno Zoo, the first national zoo in Japan, was established in 1882. Around 500 species of animals are kept in the zoo.
②You can view the popular pandas indoors through the windows of their enclosure, or as they play outside on the various installations or climb trees.
　　　室内で　　　窓越しに
　　　飼育部屋
　　　設備
③The zoo is divided into the *Ueno-no-yama* area in the east and the *Shinobazu-no-ike* area in the west. These are connected by a monorail train.
　　　　　　　　　　　　　　モノレール

---

39. 上野動物園
人気者のパンダを見に行こう！

①1882（明治15）年に開園した、日本初の公立動物園です。約500種の動物が飼育されています。
②人気のパンダ舎では、室内で飼育されている様子を窓越しに見られるほか、屋外の施設で遊んだり木に登ったりする愛らしい様子も観察できます。
③動物園は上野の山の東園と不忍池の西園に分かれ、モノレールで結ばれています。

40 The Tokyo National Museum
See the splendid architecture of Japan's first museum

①Japan's first museum, the National Museum, was established in 1872. It holds over 110000 items, including 87 National Treasures and 631 Important Cultural Properties.
②The *Hon-kan* displays Japanese works of industrial (applied) arts and historical documents. The *Tōyō-kan* displays eastern art objects and artifacts. The *Heisei-kan* displays Japanese archaeological artifacts. The Gallery of *Hōryū-ji* Treasures displays treasures donated to the *Hōryū-ji* temple.

---

40. 東京国立博物館
建物も見ものの、日本初の博物館

①1872(明治5)年に、日本初の博物館として設立されました。収蔵品は11万点以上、国宝87点、重要文化財631点を収蔵しています。
②本館は日本の美術工芸品や歴史資料、東洋館は東洋の美術と考古遺物、平成館は日本の考古遺物、法隆寺宝物館では法隆寺の献納宝物を展示しています。

41 The National Science Museum
Marvel at the 360 degree Earth model

①The National Science Museum is Japan's only fully comprehensive national science museum. The *Chikyū-kan* displays the history of life on earth and the human race. The *Nihon-kan* is devoted to nature on the Japanese archipelago and the history of the Japanese people.

②The popular 'Theater 360 (*San-roku-maru*)' features a 1:1000000 model of the Earth's interior projected on screens. From a bridge which projects out into the middle of the sphere, you have a 360 degree view on the impressive spherical panorama before you.

---

41. 国立科学博物館
360度の全天球映像は大迫力

①国立で唯一の、総合的な科学系博物館です。地球生命史と人類について展示する地球館と、日本列島の自然や日本人に関した展示の日本館からなります。②人気の「シアター360（さんろくまる）」は、地球の100万分の1の大きさの球体内部スクリーンに設けられた、中空のブリッジに立って鑑賞するもの。その名の通り360度の全天球映像が大迫力です。

42 The National Museum of Western Arts
Exhibiting western art from the late medieval period to the modern age

①The National Museum of Western Arts was opened in 1959. It holds a great number of western artworks, centering on the *Matsukata Kōjiro* collection. ②Religious paintings by Rubens and other pre-18th century artists, along with the works of representative artists from the 19th and early 20th century are all on permanent display. ③The front garden displays sculptures by Rodin, while the splendid architecture of the museum building itself was designed by the French architect Le Corbusier.

---

42. 国立西洋美術館
中世末期から近代までの西洋美術を展示

①1959（昭和34）年に開館した、松方幸次郎コレクションを中心に西洋の美術作品を多数収蔵する美術館です。②ルーベンスなど18世紀以前の宗教画をはじめ、19世紀から20世紀初頭を代表する画家の絵画も常設展示しています。③ロダンなどの彫刻が配された前庭、フランスの建築家ル・コルビュジエの設計による建物も見どころです。

43. *Yokoyama Taikan* Memorial Hall
Tracing the footsteps of the leading *Nihon-ga* painter

①The memorial hall is the house in which *Yokoyama Taikan* once lived, in *Ikenohata, Ueno*. Here you can see the *Shōko-dō* room which was used for hosting visitors, along with *Yokoyama*'s atelier and his bed room. The memorial hall also displays many of *Taikan*'s paintings.

②The *Shōko-dō* with its old Japanese style hearth and Acala (*Fudō-myōō*, designated as an Important Cultural Property) has a calm and peaceful atmosphere and offers a view out onto the garden.

---

43. 横山大観記念館
日本画壇の重鎮の足跡をたどる

①横山大観が暮らした、上野池之端の住居を利用した記念館です。客間として使用されていた鉦鼓洞や画室、寝室などの建物が見学でき、大観の作品も展示されています。
②囲炉裏や重要文化財の不動明王が配された鉦鼓洞は、庭園を眺められる落ち着いたたたずまいです。

44 The *Shitamachi* Museum
A museum of life in the good old days of downtown Tokyo

①This museum displays many old utensils and furnishings which illustrate the daily lives and culture of the ordinary people of *Shitamachi*, Tokyo's downtown area.

②On the first floor of the museum, life during the *Taishō* period is reconstructed. Here, a *nagaya* terrace house, and merchant house stand side by side. Many working tools and everyday goods are placed in these houses, and visitors can reach out and touch life in *Shitamachi* and actually step inside the reconstructed rooms.

---

44. 台東区立下町風俗資料館
古き良き下町を伝える資料館

①下町の庶民の生活や文化を後世に伝える資料館で、当時の生活道具や調度品をはじめとする下町関連の資料を展示しています。

②1階には大正時代の町並みが復元され、長屋や商家が並びます。作業道具や日用品などが配置され、実際に部屋に上がって当時の生活に触れることができます。

45

Ameyoko
The kitchen of *Shitamachi* ordinary folk, and also a place to find fashion and accessories

①This shopping street with its 430 stores is located along <u>railway tracks</u> between the JR *Okachimachi* Station and

　　　　　　　　　　　線路

Ueno. Here you will mainly find <u>fresh foodstuffs</u> on sale,

　　　　　　　　　　　　　　　　　生鮮食料品

but there are also shoes, clothes and <u>miscellaneous goods</u>

　　　　　　　　　　　　　　　　　　　　　　　雑貨

<u>at rock-bottom prices</u>.

　底価で

②If you walk through the streets here you are sure to hear

the sound of <u>salespeople</u> <u>calling out to</u> customers echoing

　　　　　　　販売員　　　～に呼びかける　　　　　　～に響き渡る

<u>through</u> this <u>lively</u> and <u>bustling</u> area: "*yasui yo!*" (it's going

　　　　　　　活気ある　　賑やかな

cheap!) or "*omake suru yo!*" (I'll give you a discount!). You

will also find fresh seafood such as <u>crab</u>, <u>tuna</u> and <u>salmon</u>,

　　　　　　　　　　　　　　　　　　カニ　マグロ　　　　サケ

as well as chocolate and foreign sweets. <u>Buy large quanti-</u>

　　　　　　　　　　　　　　　　　　　　　まとめ買いをする

<u>ties</u> in one place and you will get a good discount. During

<u>the last days of the year</u> as people prepare for the New Year

　　　年末

celebrations, the streets of *Ameyoko* become so busy that

お祝い

you <u>can hardly</u> move.

　ほとんど～できない

③For fashion and accessories we recommend the *Ameyoko*

　　　　　　　　　　　　　　　　　　　　　　　　アメ横センタービル

Center Building. There are many food stores in the underground (地下の) arcade. Here you will find Korean, Chinese, Taiwanese and Southeast Asian foods and ingredients (食材), amongst other world cuisines.

45. アメ横(よこ)
下町庶民の台所。ファッションやアクセサリーも

① JR線の御徒町(おかちまち)から上野にかけての高架線に沿って延びる商店街で、線路沿いと高架下におよそ430もの店が軒を連ねています。生鮮食料品を中心に、靴や衣類、雑貨などが、激安価格で扱われています。

② 通りを歩いていると、「安いよ！」「おまけするよ！」など、左右から威勢のいい呼び込みやたたき売りの声が響き、とても賑やかです。カニやマグロ、サケといった魚介、チョコレートや外国からのお菓子の店が目につき、まとめ買いをすればかなり割安に。正月に向けた買い出し客でごった返す年末は、身動きがとれないほどの大混雑になります。

③ ファッションやアクセサリーなら、アメ横センタービルがおすすめ。地下の食品店街にはアジア食材の店が多く、中国をはじめ韓国や台湾、東南アジアなどの食材が揃っています。

46 Yushima Temman-gū shrine
Pray for success in exams at the *Tenjinja* shrine

① *Yushima Temman-gū* is one of the foremost shrines in Tokyo dedicated to the god of learning. Its origins are said to lie with the enshrinement here (alongside another deity) of *Sugawara no Michizane* (deified as *Tenjin*, god of learning) in 1355.

② It is also known for its Japanese plum blossoms. From early February to early March a Japanese plum festival is held which attracts many visitors to the shrine.

---

46. 湯島天満宮
合格祈願の天神社

① 都内有数の学問の神様で、1355（正平10）年に菅原道真公を合祀したことが由縁とされています。
② 梅の名所でもあり、2月上旬～3月上旬には梅まつりが開かれ、境内は参拝客で賑わいを見せます。

47 *Kyū-Iwasaki-tei* Garden
A visit to the luxurious mansion of the *Mitsubishi* founder

①The former residence of the *Iwasaki* family who founded the *Mitsubishi Zaibatsu* has been opened up to the public. Built by the British architect Josiah Conder, it consists of three buildings, a Western-style building, a billiard salon, and Japanese-style building.

②The facilities and design of this mansion, such as toilet bowls in the washroom made by Royal Doulton and Japanese leather paper wallpaper. The facilities and design of this mansion offer a glimpse of the power held by the *Iwasaki* family.

---

47. 旧岩崎邸庭園
三菱の創設者の豪邸にお邪魔

①三菱財閥の創設者、岩崎家の旧邸宅を公開しており、英国の建築家であるジョサイア・コンドル設計の洋館、撞球（ビリヤード）室と和館の３棟からなります。
②ドルトン社製のトイレや金唐革紙を使用した壁紙など、邸内のさまざまなしつらえから岩崎家の力がうかがい知れます。

48 AREA GUIDE

Yanesen

①*Yanesen* takes its name from an abbreviation of the first parts of the names of the neighborhoods it represents: *Yanaka*, *Nezu*, and *Sendagi*. It is a popular area for strolling through, and it retains a strong downtown atmosphere of *Shitamachi*. This is an area that has many faces, with its small shopping streets, alleyways where ordinary people make their lives and its temple walls.

②Many famous people lie at rest in the extensive grounds of the *Yanaka Reien* Cemetery, and you will see people visiting their graves. Here you will find the tombs of the 15th and last shogun of the *Edo* shogunate *Tokugawa Yoshinobu*, the painter *Yokoyama Taikan* and the novelist *Shishi Bunroku* among others. The locations of these tombs are shown on a map of the cemetery provided by the management office.

③ *Yanesen*'s down-to-earth shopping area is also popular. In
  　　　　　　　庶民的な
the *Yanaka-ginza* shopping street and *Yomise-dōri* you will
　　谷中銀座商店街
find shops selling ready-made savory dishes and sweets,
　　　　　　　　　　惣菜
which are tempting to eat as a snack while walking through
　　　　　魅力的な
the area. The cafes and galleries in the old private and mer-
　　　　　　　　　　　　　　　　　　　　民家・商家
chant houses are the ideal spot for a break.
　　　　　　　　　　　　　　　　　休憩

48. 谷根千
エリアガイド

①谷根千とは谷中、根津、千駄木の頭文字をとった略称で、下町風情を色濃く残している、散策に人気のエリアです。商店街や庶民的な路地、寺の塀など、さまざまな表情を見せています。

②谷中霊園は広大な敷地に多くの著名人が眠っていて、それらを訪ね歩く人も目にします。江戸幕府最後の十五代将軍である徳川慶喜をはじめ、画家の横山大観、小説家の獅子文六などで、管理事務所で配布の案内図で墓所の場所が分かります。

③庶民的な商店街も人気のエリアで、谷中銀座商店街やよみせ通りには、惣菜や甘味の店が点在。歩きながらのおやつにもってこいです。昔ながらの民家や商家を利用した喫茶やギャラリーは、休憩スポットに最適です。

49

Nezu Jinja shrine
A famous spot for beautiful architecture and azaleas

①*Nezu Jinja* is one of the most famous ancient shrines in Tokyo. Its origin lies with *Yamato takeru no mikoto*, who dedicated a shrine in *Sendagi* to the god *Susanō no mikoto*.
②Many of the shrine buildings are nationally designated Important Cultural Properties. The splendid and stately architecture to be seen here includes the *gongen*-style main hall, the *heiden* hall of offerings, the *haiden* hall of worship, the *karamon* gate, the west gate, the *sukibei* fence, and the *rōmon* gate. The shrine precincts are a famous spot for azalea.

---

49. 根津神社
荘厳な建物が並ぶツツジの名所

①日本武尊が千駄木に須佐之男命をまつったことに始まる、都内有数の古社です。
②社殿は多くが重要文化財に指定され、権現造りの本殿に幣殿、拝殿、唐門、西門、透塀、楼門など、重厚かつきらびやかな造りが見ものです。境内はツツジの名所でもあります。

旅のポイント

Yūyake Dandan and the *Yanaka-ginza* shopping street
夕焼けだんだんと谷中銀座商店街

A walk from *Nippori* Station to the *Yanaka-ginza* shopping street leads you to a 36 step stairway near the entrance of the shopping street. As the name *Yūyake Dandan* (sunset steps) suggests, from the top of the stone steps, you can enjoy a beautiful view of the sun setting over the shopping street.

The *Yanaka-ginza* shopping street is known for the many cats that live there. Near *Yūyake Dandan* you will see cats basking in the sun or taking a nap. You will see many cat design art objects and cat motifs on the roofs and shop fronts in the shopping street.

The *Yanaka-ginza* shopping street is 170 meters long and has about 60 stores. The majority of these are stores with close links to the local community. Many tourists can also be seen here on weekends and during holidays.

　日暮里駅から谷中銀座商店街へ向けて歩いていくと、入口のところに36段の石段があります。「夕焼けだんだん」の名の通り、石段の上からは商店街の向こう側に、美しい夕焼けが広がるのが眺められます。

　谷中銀座商店街はネコが多いことで知られ、夕焼けだんだん付近では日なたぼっこや昼寝をするネコの姿も。

　谷中銀座商店街は、170mの通りに60軒ほどの商店が軒を連ねています。地域に密着した商店が中心で、休日には観光客の姿も多く見られます。

50 AREA GUIDE

Akihabara

①*Akihabara* is known as one the world's largest <u>electronics towns</u>. Today, *Akihabara* is a hobby town which <u>attracts</u> people <u>with interests</u> in many different genres. It <u>bustles with</u> *otaku*: people with an <u>obsessive</u> interest in <u>such things as</u> computers, *anime*, games, <u>figurine models</u> of *anime* characters, or <u>model trains</u>.

②Around the station you will find many department stores for <u>electronic products</u>. Going through the various floors, you are certain to find <u>anything you might need</u>, from <u>mobile phones</u> and <u>stereo systems</u>, to computers, TV sets, and <u>home electrical appliances</u>. You will also find large <u>specialist stores</u> <u>devoted to</u> computers or audio systems.

③*Akihabara* is also known for its Japanese *anime* and comic culture which now has many <u>devoted</u> fans both in

Japan and abroad. Walking through *Akihabara*, you may see people dressed as popular *anime* characters. The area is also known for its maid cafes where customers are welcomed by people dressed as French maids who will say "*okaerinasaimase, goshujin sama*" or "welcome home, master", a level of service you can only experience in *Akihabara*.

---

50. 秋葉原
エリアガイド

①世界有数の電気街として知られ、今ではホビーの町としてさまざまなジャンルの趣味層が集結する街となっています。パソコンにアニメやゲーム、フィギュア、鉄道模型など、「オタク」と称されるマニアで賑わっています。

②駅の周辺には、電気製品の大型店舗が並んでいます。携帯電話、オーディオ、パソコン、テレビ、家電など、一巡すれば必要なものはすべて手に入るほど。パソコンやオーディオは、全館が専門店舗となっているビルもあります。

③日本発のアニメやコミックは、今や世界中のファンを魅了する人気アイテム。町を歩けばアニメのキャラクターにコスプレした人を見かけることも。「おかえりなさいませ、ご主人さま」と迎えてくれるメイド喫茶も、秋葉原ならではのおもてなしです。

51 *Akihabara* Radio Center

A parts and accessories center worthy of electronics town *Akihabara*

①This building beneath the raised lines of *Akihabara* Station hosts many stores selling electronic parts and devices. There are more than 40 stores specializing in items such as connectors, capacitors, and plugs.
②Initially, the stores in this area sold radio parts and provided radio repair services. They were opened by radio operators returning to Japan after the war. Even today many of the stores here sell radio related items.

---

51. 秋葉原ラジオセンター

電気の町・秋葉原らしいパーツ屋街

①秋葉原駅ガード下にある電子機器や電子部品を扱う店舗が集まった建物で、コネクターやコンデンサ、プラグなど40あまりの専門店が軒を連ねています。
②もとは戦後引き揚げてきた無線技術者たちが、このあたりでラジオの部品販売や修理を行う店を開いたのが始まりで、現在も無線関係の店舗が中心です。

Travel tips

旅のポイント

Holy ground for *otaku* culture オタクの聖地

In addition to *Akihabara*, places where you can make contact with the world of Japanese *anime* (animations), *manga* (comic books), and gaming that is called '*otaku* culture' include *Nakano* Broadway and *Otome* Road.

Nakano Broadway, which is just past the *Nakano* Sun Mall shopping area that stands in front of the north entrance to *Nakano* Station, is filled with shops specializing in a wide variety of different genres of *manga*, *anime* and other *otaku* products. The huge used book chain store *Mandarake* is at the top of the list. In recent years, *Nakano* has become so much of an *otaku* holy land that people have come to say '*Akihabara* in the west, *Nakano* in the east'. *Otome* Road, next to the East Gate of *Ikebukuro*, is a holy land for *fujoshi* (female *otaku*). Many of the stores there are aimed at women. These include *Mandarake*, Animate Sunshine, and 'butler' cafes.

　秋葉原のほかにも、日本のアニメや漫画、ゲームなどいわゆる「オタク文化」に触れられる場所として、中野ブロードウェイや乙女(おとめ)ロードがあります。

　中野駅北口正面に位置する商店街・中野サンモールの先にある中野ブロードウェイは、巨大古書チェーンの「まんだらけ」を筆頭に、漫画やアニメなどの幅広いジャンルの店が揃っています。近年、「西の秋葉原、東の中野」といわれるほどのオタクの聖地になっています。また、池袋東口側の乙女ロードは、腐女子(女性のオタク)の聖地です。店舗の多くが女性向けで、まんだらけやアニメイトサンシャインをはじめ執事喫茶などがあります。

52 AREA GUIDE

Kanda, Jimbōchō

①This area is known for the *Kanda myōjin*, a shrine associated with the three great festivals of *Edo* (江戸三大祭り), the Byzantine style (ビザンチン様式) church Nicholai-*dō*, and the *Yushima-seidō*, the site of a Confucian academy (儒学の学問所) established by *Tokugawa Tsunayoshi*, 5th shogun of the *Edo* shogunate (江戸幕府). In addition to the student district (学生街) and the used book (古本) district, between *Ochanomizu* and *Kanda/Jimbōchō* there are many stores selling musical instruments (楽器) and sports equipment.

②The *Kanda* area retains (〜を保つ) the style of the old city as it escaped destruction in the war (戦災). The *Awajichō* and *Sudachō* areas offer many old-style restaurants. Along the *Nishiguchi-shōtengai* shopping street you will also find many bars serving *yakitori* (焼き鳥) grilled chicken and *kushiyaki* (串焼き) skewer dishes (料理). At night this area bustles with (〜で賑わう) Japanese white collar workers drawn to the red lanterns of the popular bars and restaurants.

③ *Kanda ko-shōtengai* is Japan's largest used books district, with more than 200 book stores. Most stores specialize in one particular genre. As this is a student area, many stores offer academic books.

---

52. 神田・神保町
エリアガイド

①江戸三大祭りゆかりの神田明神に、ビザンチン様式の教会のニコライ堂、江戸幕府5代将軍徳川綱吉が開いた学問所跡に建つ湯島聖堂、さらに学生街に古書街、楽器屋とスポーツ用品店が集まるお茶の水〜神保町界隈など、歴史と文化の色合いが濃いエリアです。

②神田界隈は戦災を免れた古い街並みが残っており、淡路町や須田町には昔ながらの店構えで営業している食事処もあります。また西口商店街には焼き鳥や串焼きなど庶民派の居酒屋が建ち並び、日が暮れると赤ちょうちんに誘われたサラリーマンで賑わいます。

③神田古書店街は日本で最大規模の古本屋街で、200軒あまりの古書店が軒を連ねています。ほとんどの店が専門のジャンルを持っており、学生街という場所柄、学術書の品揃えが豊富です。

53

Isegen
A popular restaurant for anglerfish dishes established in the *Edo*-period

①*Isegen* is located in *Kanda Sudachō*. It specializes in ang-
～を専門にする
lerfish dishes, and has a history of more than 180 years.
アンコウ料理
This restaurant was built in 1930, and features a traditional

Japanese shop signboard.
屋台入り看板
②*Isegen* is famous for *ankō-nabe* (anglerfish meat served
身
hot with vegetables in a pot) served with the restaurant's

legendary secret *warishita* seasoning sauce. It is also
秘伝の　　　　　　　　　　味付けソース
known for its flour-coated fried items and jellied broth. As
唐揚げ　　　　　　　　煮こごり
the anglerfish is very fresh, you can also enjoy its meat and
新鮮な
liver sliced raw, as *sashimi*.

---

53. いせ源(げん)
江戸期に創業のアンコウ料理の老舗

①神田須田町(かんだすだちょう)に店を構える、約180年もの歴史を持つアンコウ料理の専門店です。年季の入った屋号入り看板が掲げられた建物は、1930（昭和5）年建築の趣ある一軒家です。②秘伝の割下で味わうあんこう鍋が名物のほか、唐揚げや煮こごり、さらに鮮度のいいアンコウを使うため身や肝を刺身で味わうことができます。

54

Takemura
A Japanese traditional sweets shop which appears in works by the author *Ikenami Shōtarō*

①This sweets shop (甘味処), built in 1930 in *Kanda Sudachō*, was popular with the writer (作家) *Ikenami Shōtarō*.
②The *Takemura* store is a designated historical building (選定歴史的建造物) of the city of Tokyo. It retains (〜を保つ), with its *irimoya-zukuri* (a hip-and-gable roof construction), the feel (たたずまい) of the *Shōwa* (昭和) period.
③The store is most famous for its *awa zenzai*, a dish which uses millet (粟) steamed in a basket (せいろ), and its deep fried *age manjū* cakes.

54. 竹むら
池波正太郎の作品にも登場する甘味処

①1930（昭和5）年創業の神田須田町にある甘味処で、作家の池波正太郎がひいきにしていたお店です。
②東京都の選定歴史的建造物に指定されている建物は、重厚感が感じられる入母屋造りで、昭和のたたずまいを随所に残しています。
③せいろでていねいに蒸した粟を使った粟ぜんざい、揚げたてを店内でいただく揚げまんじゅうが名物です。

旅のポイント

Relaxing at a *sentō* bathhouse
銭湯でゆったりくつろぐ
せんとう

In the old downtown district of Tokyo many of the old-fashioned public bathhouses known as *sentō* still exist today. After entering the bathhouse through traditional *noren* sign curtains a small fee is to be paid before you can enjoy a hot bath while gazing at large wall paintings. The public bathhouses are the essential relaxation spot to make for after a walk through the old downtown areas of *Shitamachi*.

Some of the *sentō* bathhouses are built in the style of old Japanese architecture. These are splendid old-fashioned wood buildings in shrine-style architecture with *karahafu* (cusped gable) roofs and shelves with coffered ceilings. The wall paintings or mosaics often display scenes of Mt. *Fuji*, lakes or coasts. One can gaze at this 'magnificent scenery' while taking a hot bath.

　東京下町エリアには、昔ながらの公衆浴場「銭湯」が、今もなおたくさん残っています。暖簾をくぐって番台で入浴料を払い、大きな壁画を眺めながら広々した湯船でくつろぐ。下町散策には欠かせないリラクセーションスポットです。

　銭湯の建物には、昔ながらの重厚な和風建築のものがあります。宮型造りの建物や唐破風の屋根、格天井に透かし彫りが施された欄間など、木造建築としても見どころが豊富です。ペンキ絵やタイル画の壁画は、富士山や湖や海岸といった景勝を描いていて、"雄大な風景"を眺めながらの入浴が楽しめます。

Chapter 4

Downtown Tokyo

第4章
東京の繁華街

55 AREA GUIDE

Odaiba

①*Odaiba* takes its name from the fact that a marine battery (洋上砲台) was placed here by the shogunate (幕府) during the *Edo* period (江戸時代) to repel (〜を追い返す) foreign ships. From the *Meiji* period (明治時代) onward, land reclamation (埋め立て) in the area has been carried out. Moreover, from the end of the *Shōwa* period (昭和) and into the *Heisei* period (平成), a project was put into practice (実行された) to develop the area as a coastal subcenter of Tokyo (臨海副都心).

②Now, there are a range of amusement facilities (アミューズメント施設) along the *Rinkai* Line (りんかい線) between the Tokyo Teleport and *Kokusai-tenjijō* Stations, and along the *Yurikamome* Line (ゆりかもめ線) between the *Odaiba-kaihinkōen* and *Ariake*-tennis-*no-mori* Stations.

③The area is so rich (充実している) with shopping malls, outlet malls, hot springs, and museums that it wouldn't be possible to go around everything in just one day. The key thing is to first choose the places you want to visit, and walk around with that area as your focus. Of course, it is also a new tourist spot where it's enjoyable enough to just take a carefree stroll along the seashore, or simply gaze at the sunset.

---

55. お台場
エリアガイド

① もともとは江戸時代、幕府が異国船打払いのために洋上砲台を設置したのが名前の由来です。明治期以降も周辺の埋め立てが進められ、さらに昭和末から平成にかけて、臨海副都心として開発計画が進められました。

② 現在は、りんかい線なら東京テレポート駅から国際展示場駅、ゆりかもめならお台場海浜公園駅から有明テニスの森駅までの間に、いろいろなアミューズメント施設がそろっています。

③ ショッピングモール、アウトレット、温泉、博物館と、とても1日では回りきれない充実度。遊びたい施設をまず決めて、そのエリアを中心に歩くのがポイント。もちろん、ただのんびりと海辺を散策したり、夕日を眺めたりするだけでも充分楽しめる、東京の新名所です。

56 *Ōedo Onsen Monogatari*
A natural hot spring you can enjoy at *Odaiba*

① A Japanese-style garden of 2310 square meters in this hot springs facility has a walking path beside a 50 meter long hot water foot spa, and open-air baths. There is plenty to do here for a whole day's enjoyment.

② This natural hot spring, which is drawn up from 1400 meters underground, is a sodium-chloride strong saline spring. It is effective for relieving muscle pain and poor circulation, and will warm you all the way to the core.

- A Japanese-style garden — 日本庭園
- hot water foot spa — 足湯
- open-air baths — 露天風呂
- natural hot spring — 天然温泉
- drawn up — 汲み上げられた
- sodium-chloride strong saline spring — ナトリウム－塩化物強塩泉
- muscle pain — 筋肉痛
- poor circulation — 冷え症

---

56. 大江戸温泉物語
お台場で楽しむ天然温泉

①700坪の日本庭園には全長50mの湯の道を歩く足湯や、露天風呂などが揃っていて、1日中楽しめる温泉施設です。
②地下1400mから汲み上げた天然温泉は「ナトリウム－塩化物強塩泉」。筋肉痛や冷え症にも効能があり、体を芯からぽかぽか温めてくれる効果もあります。

第4章 ● 東京の繁華街

57 *Miraikan* (National Museum of Emerging Science and Innovation)
Make contact with the latest science and technology

① This is a museum where you can learn about the modern world from the viewpoint of science.

② The permanent display comprises three themes: '*TSUNAGARI*', which explains about all the forms of life and environments on the earth; 'Explore the Frontiers', which explains the structures of the world; and 'Create Your Future', which helps you consider 'richness' via topics such as technological innovation and robot development.

---

57. 日本科学未来館
最新の科学技術に触れてみる

① 現在の世界を科学の視点から知る博物館です。

② 常設展は、地球上のあらゆる生命や環境を解説する「つながり」、世界の仕組みを解説する「世界をさぐる」、技術革新やロボット開発などから「豊かさ」を考える「未来をつくる」の3テーマで構成されています。

58 Rainbow Bridge
Enjoy a stroll above the sea

①This suspension bridge connects the heart of Tokyo and the coastal subcenter. From dusk, the bridge is lit up with rainbow colors or colors to match the seasons. It is 798 meters in length, and Route 11 of the *Shuto* Expressway, the *Yurikamome* Line, and the *Rinkō* Road all run along this bridge.

②There is also a 1.7 kilometer promenade. From the south side of the bridge you can see *Odaiba* and Tokyo Bay, and from the north side you can view *Harumi* Wharf and almost all of the Rainbow Bridge itself.

---

58. レインボーブリッジ
海の上のお散歩を楽しもう

①都心と臨海副都心を結ぶ吊り橋。夕刻以降は虹色や季節に合わせた色にライトアップされます。長さは798mで高速11号線やゆりかもめ、臨港道路が通っています。②また橋上には約1.7kmの遊歩道があり、南側からはお台場や東京港が、北側からは晴海ふ頭や橋のほぼ全景を眺められます。

旅のポイント

Yurikamome ゆりかもめ

This new automated transportation system began operating in 1995. It now connects 16 stations along a 15-kilometer line from *Shimbashi* Station to *Toyosu* Station via the *Odaiba* area in a total run of a little over 30 minutes. All of the track is elevated, and part of its appeal is that you can enjoy the view of Tokyo Bay and *Odaiba* from the train windows.

Our recommended seating area would be near the driver's seat in either in the front or rear car of the 6-car train. You can enjoy a panoramic view through the windows at the front (or rear) and the sides of the train.

　1995年に開業した無人運転の新交通システム。現在は新橋駅からお台場地区を経由して、豊洲駅の間の15km16駅を30分強で結んでいます。専用の軌道はすべて高架で、東京港やお台場の景色が楽しめる車窓風景が魅力のひとつ。

　おすすめの乗車位置は、6両編成の先頭か最後尾の車両の運転席。前方（後方）と左右に広がる車窓パノラマを楽しめます。

59 AREA GUIDE

Roppongi

①*Roppongi* is an area dominated by two building complexes (複合施設), huge even for Tokyo: the 238-meter-tall *Roppongi* Hills and the 248-meter-tall Tokyo Midtown. It is also crowded with (〜がひしめく) restaurants with a markedly international character (国際色豊かな). From around 1965 onward, this area developed as a night spot where many foreigners gathered and entertainers (芸能人) made frequent appearances (出没する), but in recent years, it has prospered (栄えた) as a district that you can enjoy not only at night, but also during the day.

②This area stretches out (広がる) from its center at *Roppongi* Intersection (六本木交差点), where *Roppongi* Boulevard (六本木通り) (Route 3 of the *Shuto* Expressway) (首都高速3号線) and *Gaien* East Boulevard (外苑東通り) meet.

③The highlights (見どころ) of this area are, of course, *Roppongi* Hills and Tokyo Midtown. These buildings host the *Mori* Art (森美術館)

第4章●東京の繁華街

Museum and the Suntory Museum of Art (respectively),
　　　　　　　サントリー美術館　　　　　　　それぞれ
and if you follow a walking course that combines them with The National Art Center, you can enjoy an entire day
　　　　　　　国立新美術館
absorbed in art.
アート三昧

59. 六本木(ろっぽんぎ)
エリアガイド

①高さ238mの六本木ヒルズと248mの東京ミッドタウンという、東京でも有数の巨大な複合施設と、国際色豊かな飲食店がひしめく六本木。1965（昭和40）年頃以降、外国人が多く集まり、芸能人も出没するナイトスポットとして発展しましたが、近年は夜だけでなく昼も楽しめる街として賑わっています。

②街は、首都高速3号線が通る六本木通りと外苑(がいえん)東通りが交わる六本木交差点を中心に広がっています。

③見どころはやはり六本木ヒルズと東京ミッドタウン。それぞれに森美術館とサントリー美術館があり、国立新美術館と組み合わせたお散歩ルートをたどれば、アート三昧の1日が楽しめます。

60 *Roppongi* Hills
An open-air deck 270 meters above sea level

①Various features (機能), including offices, residences, cultural facilities, a hotel, and a TV station (テレビ局), are condensed into (〜に集約されている) a plot (敷地) the size of eight Tokyo Domes. Among them are the ultra-famous (超有名) French restaurant L'Atelier de Joël Robuchon and the Armani Jeans / Armani Junior boutique. Stepping outside the building, high-class brand shops such as Armani and Tiffany line (軒を連ねる) *Roppongi Keyakizaka* Boulevard (六本木けやき坂通り).

②The green which is richly arranged around the various areas within the facility is also appealing (魅力的). The *Mōri* Garden (毛利庭園) is built on the site where *Mōri Hidemoto* built his residence (屋敷) in 1650. *Hidemoto* was the grandson of *Mōri Motonari*, the warlord (大名) who conquered Japan's *Chūgoku* region (中国地方) during Japan's Warring States (*Sengoku*) period. This garden is particularly worth seeing (一見の価値あり).

③The places in this area that are absolutely not to be (はずせない)

120

missed are Tokyo City View on the 52nd floor and Sky Deck on the building's rooftop. The Sky Deck, as it is located 270 meters above sea level, offers a particularly impressive and unobstructed view of Tokyo.

60. 六本木ヒルズ
海抜270mのオープンエアデッキ

①東京ドーム8個分の敷地に、オフィス・住居・文化施設・ホテル・テレビ局など、さまざまな機能が集約されています。中には超有名フレンチレストラン「ラトリエ ジョエル・ロブション」や「アルマーニ・ジーンズ／アルマーニ・ジュニア」ブティックも。ビルから一歩外へ出た六本木けやき坂通りには「アルマーニ」「ティファニー」などの高級ブランドブティックが軒を連ねています。

②施設内の各所に豊かに配置されている緑も魅力です。特に1650(慶安3)年、戦国時代の中国地方の覇者・毛利元就の孫の秀元が設けた大名屋敷の庭園跡地にある「毛利庭園」は一見の価値があります。

③何といってもはずせないのが、52階の東京シティビューと建物屋上のスカイデッキ。特にスカイデッキは海抜270mに位置し、遮るもののない東京の展望を楽しめます。

61 Tokyo Midtown
A base for touring *Roppongi* art

①This multi-facility urban complex (複合施設) has an above-ground 54-story building (地上54階建) at its center that was constructed on the site of the suburban residence (下屋敷) of the *Mōri* clan (毛利家) feudal lords of the *Chōshū* domain (長州藩). From the *Meiji* period (明治時代) onward this area was an army post (陸軍駐屯地), then, after World War II (第二次世界大戦), it was used as lodging quarters (宿舎) for the US military (米軍). After being returned to Japan, it was a government office building for the Japan Defense Agency (防衛庁), but development began in 2000 and this complex opened in 2007.

②It is made up of (〜からなる) shops, restaurants, hotels, housing, museums and the like, and it is bordered by the lushly green (緑豊かな) *Minato* Ward *Hinokichō* Park (港区立檜町公園). Tokyo Midtown is fairly close (程近い) to The National Art Center, and it can be nice to (〜するのもいいもの) stop around here for a meal or tea before or after viewing some artwork.

③At the center of the shopping area is the Galleria, with its

pleasant 150-meter-long, 25-meter-high atrium, and the
　　気持ちいい　　　　　　　　　　　　　　　　　　　　　吹き抜け空間

Plaza, with its expansive glass ceiling. The shopping area is

situated from the first basement floor to the fourth floor.

61. 東京ミッドタウン
六本木アート巡りの拠点にも

① 長州藩毛利家下屋敷跡に建つ、地上54階建のビルを中心とした複合施設。明治期以降は陸軍駐屯地に、第二次大戦後は一時期米軍宿舎、さらに返還後は防衛庁の庁舎でしたが、2000（平成12）年から開発が始まり2007（平成19）年にオープンしました。

② ショップ、レストラン、ホテル、住居、美術館などからなり、緑豊かな港区立檜町公園に隣接しています。国立新美術館に程近く、芸術鑑賞の前後に食事やお茶で立ち寄るのもいいもの。

③ ショッピングエリアは全長150m、高さ25mの吹き抜け空間が気持ちいいガレリアと、ガラス天井で開放的なプラザを中心に、建物の地下1階から4階に設けられています。

62 Tokyo Tower
The symbol of Japan's postwar period of rapid growth

①At 333 meters in height, Tokyo Tower has passed on the mantle of tallest tower to the 634-meter-tall Tokyo Skytree, but ever since it opened in 1958, it is safe to say that there has been no change in its status as a symbol of Tokyo and Japan's postwar period of rapid growth.

②As its official name *Nippon Denpa-tō* (Radio Tower) implies, it was originally a radio tower for broadcasting various kinds of radio frequencies throughout Tokyo. However, as there are no buildings of comparable height in its location in the *Minato* Ward in the center of Tokyo, the view from the 250-meter-high special observation deck is still popular as a splendid tourist spot. Not only is the view enjoyable, but the lighting up of Tokyo Tower itself which colors it according to the seasons and for various events has become a feature of Tokyo.

③Something that you may find interesting inside the tower

building is underline(the Tokyo Tower Aquarium) in Foot Town. 50,000
　　　　　　　東京タワー水族館
fish representing 900 different species from around the
world are on display, and it is a very underline(calming) place.
　　　展示されている　　　　　　　　　　　　　落ち着く

62. 東京タワー
日本高度成長期のシンボル

①333mと高さでこそ634mの東京スカイツリーに譲りましたが、1958（昭和33）年の開業以来東京の、いや日本高度成長期のシンボル的存在であることに変わりないでしょう。
②本来は正式名称の「日本電波塔」が示す通り、さまざまな種類の電波が東京中に届くようにする電波塔でした。しかし東京都心の港区に位置し周囲には比較的高い建物がないことから、今でも250mの特別展望台からの眺望は、絶好の観光スポットとして相変わらず人気です。展望が楽しめるだけでなく、東京タワー自体もライトアップによって季節やイベントなどによりさまざまに彩られ、東京の風物詩となっています。
③館内でちょっと面白いのが、フットタウンにある東京タワー水族館。世界中の900種類5万匹の観賞魚が展示されていて、とてもなごめる空間です。

63 AREA GUIDE

Azabu Jūban

①*Azabu Jūban* is a part of town which offers traditional Tokyo downtown atmosphere [下町風情] in its shopping area, close through it is to the modern *Roppongi* Hills tower building. You can enjoy the juxtaposition [並んでいること] of old and new in *Roppongi*. Even if you walk at a leisurely [ゆっくりとした] pace from *Roppongi* Hills, it will only take you [〜(時間)しかかからない] about 20 minutes to get through the main street, where even the side roads [路地] which stretch out to the left and right are lined with unique [個性的な] shops.

②From a temple town [門前町] that developed around *Azabusan Zenpuku-ji* temple [麻布山善福寺], which is said to [〜と伝えられる] have been founded in 824, the *Azabu Jūban* neighborhood [界隈] started to prosper during the *Edo* period [江戸時代] as it became lined with many feudal lords' [大名] suburban residences [下屋敷]. Still, the allure [魅力] of the area stems from its numerous long-established shops [老舗] that pre-

serve traces of the past.
    往時の面影
③Along with the *soba* (buckwheat noodle) restaurants *Azabu Nagasaka Sarashina Honten* and *Sōhonke Sarashina Horii* and the *taiyaki* (fish-shaped pancake filled with bean paste) shop *Naniwaya Sōhonten*, there are many other well-established shops in the area.
              老舗

---

63. 麻布十番
エリアガイド

①六本木ヒルズの程近くに、こんな下町風情が感じられる街並みが！ というギャップも楽しい昔ながらの商店街。六本木ヒルズからのんびりと散歩しても、20分程度で抜けてしまう通りを中心に、左右に延びる路地にも、個性的なお店が軒を連ねています。

②824（天長元）年創建と伝えられる麻布山善福寺の門前町から、江戸時代には多くの大名の下屋敷が建ち並び、賑わい始めた麻布十番界隈。やはりその魅力は、往時の面影を残す老舗の数々でしょう。

③そば屋の「麻布永坂更科本店」や「総本家更科堀井」、たい焼きの「浪花家総本店」ほか、まだまだたくさんの老舗があります。

Travel tips

Visiting the art museums of *Roppongi*
六本木の美術館巡り

Roppongi has for some time had many small but unique boutiques, but it is now popular as an art district. If you tour The National Art Center, the Suntory Museum of Art, and the *Mori* Art Museum, you can immerse yourself in various different kinds of art over the course of a single day.

■The National Art Center

This is an art museum that specializes in displaying special exhibitions and exhibitions of works by the general public rather than a permanent collection, and so it is best to check the museum's schedule before coming here. It is worth viewing not only the exhibitions, but also the building itself, with its glass facade designed by the leading Japanese architect *Kurokawa Kishō*. Brasserie Paul Bocuse Le Musée, a restaurant built to look as if it is floating in the enormous atrium of the museum, will certainly make an impression.

■Suntory Museum of Art (in Tokyo Midtown)

This museum owns works of art that are closely related to everyday life, including items such as china, porcelain, glasswork and dyeing and weaving work from the East and West. You can also observe items from their collection that are put on display in connection with special exhibitions.

■*Mori* Art Museum (in *Roppongi* Hills)

An extensive variety of modern art is on display as part of special exhibitions. The MAM Project, through which the *Mori* Art Museum supports noteworthy artists from around the world, is particularly worth a look.

旅のポイント

　以前から、小さいけれど個性的なブティックが多かった六本木ですが、今やアートの街としても人気です。国立新美術館〜サントリー美術館〜森美術館と回れば、1日中さまざまなアートにどっぷり浸れます。

■国立新美術館

　常設展示はなく企画展と公募展に特化した美術館なので、スケジュールを確認してから出かけたいところ。展覧会だけでなく、日本を代表する建築家黒川紀章(くろかわきしょう)氏が手掛けた前面がガラス張りの建物も、一見の価値があります。とくに、巨大な吹き抜け空間に浮かぶようにしつらえられたレストラン「ブラスリー ポール・ボキューズ ミュゼ」には驚かされます。

■サントリー美術館（東京ミッドタウン内）

　陶磁器や東西のガラス・染織など生活に密着した美術品を所蔵。企画展のテーマに合わせて収蔵品も展示され、鑑賞することができます。

■森美術館（六本木ヒルズ内）

　幅広い現代アートを企画展で展示。とくに森美術館が世界中の注目アーティストを応援するMAMプロジェクトは要チェックです。

64 AREA GUIDE

Shinjuku

①During the *Edo* period, the *Kōshū* Highway developed as a road connecting *Edo* with the areas of *Shinshū* and *Kōshū*, which are equivalent to the present-day prefectures of *Nagano* and *Yamanashi*. The first post station from *Edo*'s *Nihombashi* was *Takaido*, but because of the distance, a new post station, which was *Naitō Shinjuku*, was later established. This post station town expanded to become one of Japan's foremost commercial centers.

②*Shinjuku* is roughly divided into three areas: *Kabuki-chō* and the area around *Shinjuku* East Gate, the area on either side of the JR *Yamanote* Line which has historically been a 'gay quarter'; *Shinjuku* West Gate, the high-rise building area which emerged after the site of the *Yodobashi* Filtration Plant was developed; and *Shinjuku* South Gate, the

south side of the *Kōshū* Highway which straddles the JR
跨ぐ

train lines where construction on the station building and

surrounding facilities is being carried out.
周辺設備

64. 新宿(しんじゅく)
エリアガイド

①江戸時代に、今の長野県・山梨県にあたる信州・甲州と江戸を結ぶ街道として発展した甲州街道。江戸日本橋から最初の宿場が当初は高井戸でしたが、距離があるため、後から設けられたのが新しい宿場の「内藤新宿」です。この宿場町が発展して、日本でも屈指の繁華街となりました。
②新宿はおおまかに3つのエリアに分けられます。JR山手線の線路を挟んで、昔からの繁華街だった歌舞伎町と新宿東口一帯。淀橋浄水場跡地が整備されて高層ビル街が出現した新宿西口。甲州街道の南側、JRの線路をまたいで現在も駅舎や周辺設備の工事が進められている新宿南口です。

65 The Tokyo Metropolitan Government Office and the high-rise buildings of the west gate
One of the major high-rise districts in Tokyo

①In 1898, the *Yodobashi* Filtration Plant, the newest style of modern filtration facility of its time, was built here. It supported the everyday lives of Tokyo residents until 1965. The current cityscape and high-rise buildings of the *Shinjuku* West Gate zone were built on the area redeveloped around the site of that plant.

②The cityscape is made up of the area near *Shinjuku* Station where shops full of local color are crowded together, and, in contrast to that area, the systematically re-zoned high-rise building district.

③All of those buildings have restaurants or other shops in the higher floors that command fine views, but we recommend the observation rooms in the Tokyo Metropolitan Government Office. There are rooms in both the North and South Buildings, and from either of them, you can enjoy a nearly 360-degree view at 202 meters free of charge.

④We recommend the southern observation room, with its particularly good view of *Haneda* and *Yokohama*.

65. 都庁と西口高層ビル群
東京でも指折りの高層ビルの街

①1898（明治31）年、当時最新式の近代的浄水施設として淀橋浄水場が造られ、1965（昭和40）年まで都民の生活を支えました。その跡地を中心に再開発して造られたのが、今の新宿西口一帯の街並みと高層ビル群です。

②街並みは、新宿駅近くの庶民的な店が密集するエリアと、そのエリアとは対照的な計画的に区画整理された高層ビル街からなっています。

③どのビルの階上にも展望の利く飲食店などが入っていますが、おすすめは東京都庁舎の展望室。北棟と南棟両方にあり、どちらも高さ202mから、ほぼ360度の眺めが無料で楽しめます。

④とくに羽田・横浜方面の眺めがよい、南展望室がおすすめです。

66 Golden District

An air of the *Shōwa* period fills this district of intellectual

①This is a district lined with old two- and three-story wooden houses. It formed after the end of the war, when a street stall market sprung up beside the *Hanazono Jinja* shrine on the east side of *Shinjuku* Station, becoming a red-light district, and then evolving into a meeting place for intellectuals. Stepping into this area takes you back in time by several decades.

②Most of the more than 250 bars here are small, counter-only bars that are full at just 10 customers.

---

66. ゴールデン街
昭和の香り漂う文化人の街

①木造2階建て3階建ての古びた建物が軒を連ねる街。終戦後、新宿東側の花園神社脇にできた露店マーケットが始まりで、色町に、そして文化人の溜り場へと姿を変えました。この街に一歩踏み込めば、時を何十年もさかのぼれます。
②250軒以上ある飲み屋のほとんどは、カウンターのみの小さな店で、10人も入れば満席です。

67

Omoide Yokochō
An easygoing part of town where lunchtime drinks are OK!

① This drinking district preserves a strong atmosphere of
　　　飲み屋街

the street stall market that first emerged ruins of world war
　　　　　　　　　　　　　　　　　　　　　　　　戦後の焼け跡

II on the west side of *Shinjuku* Station.

② Tempted by the pleasant aroma of grilled offal, you enter
　　　　　　　　いい匂い　　　　　　　もつ焼き

a narrow alley sandwiched between buildings that are diffi-
　　　　　路地

cult to distinguish as either separate or in rows where you
　　　区別する　　　　　　　　　一軒家　　　　　長屋

find rows of shops with counters not even

big enough to seat 10 people.

---

67. 思い出横丁
昼飲みOK! の大らかな街

①終戦後の新宿西口の焼け跡にいち早く出現した露店マーケットの雰囲気を色濃く残す飲み屋街です。

②もつ焼きのいい匂いに誘われて、長屋なのか一軒家なのかも判然としない建物に挟まれた狭い路地を入ると、10人も入れないようなカウンターだけの店がずらり。

Shinjuku Imperial Garden
A genuine oasis in the metropolis

①This is a spacious park built on the site of the *Edo* residence of *Naitō Kiyonari*, a retainer of *Tokugawa Ieyasu*, which was bestowed upon him by the shogunate. ②The traditional Japanese *chisen-kaiyū* pond-centered garden, French formal garden, and English landscape garden are skillfully combined. Here you can experience nature from season to season in the center of the metropolis. There is an entrance fee.

---

68. 新宿御苑
正真正銘、都会のオアシス

①江戸時代、徳川家康の家臣だった内藤清成が幕府から拝領した、江戸屋敷跡地に造られた広々とした公園です。②池泉回遊式日本庭園、フランス式整形庭園、イギリス式風景庭園が巧みに組み合わされており、四季折々の自然を都会の真ん中で味わえます。入園は有料。

69 *Shinjuku Suehirotei*
Big laughs and powerful emotions through traditional storytelling

①The *Rakugo Iromono Teiseki Yose* is a traditional storytellers' theater for *rakugo* and other entertainment, built in 1897. You will find it past the *Shinjuku* Branch of the *Isetan* Department Store at the east entrance to *Shinjuku* Station, across *Meiji* Boulevard and just up a side street.
②This wooden building, with its paper lanterns and hand-written signboards, recreates the elegance of traditional theater as it was in days gone by.

69. 新宿末廣亭
伝統話芸に大笑い、大感動

①1897（明治30）年創業の伝統的な落語色物定席寄席。新宿東口のデパート伊勢丹新宿店の先、明治通りを渡って裏通りに入ったところにあります。
②建物は木造で提灯や手書きの看板が、昔ながらの寄席風情を醸し出しています。

70 AREA GUIDE

Shin-Ōkubo

①Tokyo's largest Korean town is located in a district just past the northern side of *Shinjuku*'s *Kabukichō*, bordered by the large thoroughfare streets (大通り) of *Ōkubo-dōri* to the north, *Meiji-dōri* to the east, *Otakibashi-dōri* to the west, and *Shokuan-dōri* to the south. Korean language (ハングル) signage (看板) catches the eye (人の目を引く) and there are numerous restaurants serving Korean home-style cooking (家庭料理).

②First time visitors may want to start from JR *Sōbu* Line's (JR総武線) *Ōkubo* Station and proceed on foot (徒歩で) towards JR *Yamanote* Line's (JR山手線) *Shin-Ōkubo* Station. Korean language signs become more apparent (目立つ) the closer one gets to *Shin-Ōkubo* Station.

③Fans of *Hanryū* (Korean pop culture) stars should head to the *Hanryū* department store (韓流百貨店) next to *Shin-Ōkubo* Station. Inside are shops selling a variety of *Hanryū* merchandise (韓流グッズ)

dise including calendars, mugs, and photo collections, and
　　　　　　　　　　　　　　　　　　　写真集
one is bound to find products dedicated to their favorite
　　　　　　　　　　　　　　　　　　　　　　　　お気に入りの
star. There is also a wide assortment of items such as
　　　　　　　　　幅広い品揃え
Korean food products and Korean cosmetics.

70. 新大久保
エリアガイド

①北は大久保通り、東は明治通り、西は小滝橋通り、南は職安通りより少し新宿寄りの歌舞伎町の北側の一帯は、東京の一大コリアンタウンです。韓国家庭料理店が軒を連ね、ハングルで書かれた看板が目立ちます。

②初めて訪れるなら、JR総武線大久保駅からJR山手線新大久保駅方面への散策がおすすめ。とくに新大久保駅に近くなればなるほど、ハングルの看板が目立つようになります。

③もし韓流スターのファンなら、新大久保駅のすぐそばの韓流百貨店へ。店内はカレンダー、マグカップ、写真集など、韓流スターグッズでいっぱいで、お目当てのスターのグッズもきっと見つけられます。ほかにも韓国食品、韓流コスメなどグッズが揃っています。

71 AREA GUIDE

Kagurazaka

①In the <u>*Edo* period</u> *Kagurazaka* was an area with many
   江戸時代

samurai residences and temples <u>side by side</u>, but <u>the *Ushi-*</u>
武家屋敷   並んで

<u>*gome geisha* district</u> was established around the end of that
牛込花街

period, and during <u>the *Meiji* period</u> the area further devel-
                    明治時代

oped into pleasure quarters known as *karyūkai*, 'the flower

and willow world' of the *geisha*.

②Even now this is a place for <u>authentic</u> Japanese cuisine in
                                 本格的な

top class restaurants where people can enjoy forms of

<u>entertainment</u> such as the songs and dances of *geisha*.
接待

Many of these places, however, <u>do not accept new custo-</u>
                                 いちげんさんお断り

<u>mers without introductions</u>.

③Small alleys branch out from the left and right sides of the

center <u>hill path</u> <u>commonly known as</u> *Kagurazaka-dōri*.
       坂道   通称

Going further down many of these alleys leads to even

more narrow stone paved pathways and stone staircases.
　　　　　　　石畳　　　　　　　　　　　　　　石段
Strolling along these paths affords a subtle taste of the ele-
そぞろ歩く　　　　　　　　　　　　　　繊細な
gant atmosphere of a *geisha* district.
風情

71. 神楽坂(かぐらざか)
エリアガイド

---

①江戸時代には武家屋敷や寺院が多く立ち並ぶ地域でしたが、江戸末期に牛込花街(うしごめはなまち)ができ、明治期に花柳界(かりゅうかい)として発展しました。
②今でも本格的な料亭があり、芸者さんの唄や踊りなどの接待を楽しむことができます。ただし原則として「いちげんさんお断り」です。
③通称・神楽坂通りの坂道を中心に、左右に路地が延びています。奥に進み、さらに石畳あり石段ありの細い路地が入り組む街並み(はなまち)をそぞろ歩けば、花街風情(はなまちふぜい)をそこはかとなく味わえるでしょう。

AREA GUIDE

Shibuya

①The 'pedestrian scramble' intersection [スクランブル交差点] just before *Hachikō* has become a symbol of Tokyo to foreign travelers and the *Shibuya* townscape [都会の風景] seems to radiate outward [放射状に広がる] from nearby *Hachikō* Square [ハチ公前広場].

②The liveliest [一番賑やか] area is *Sentā-gai* (commonly known as Basketball Street) with its series of restaurants and bars that line the road [軒を連ねる], as well as the parallel [並行する] road that is the beginning of *Inokashira-dōri*. The area in the direction of the *Shibuya Seibu* Department store [西武渋谷店], from the fashion apparel building [ファッションビル] *SHIBUYA*109 to *Bunkamura-dōri*, bustles with [〜で賑わう] people well into the night.

③One of the best things about *Shibuya* is that adults can enjoy the area as well as teenagers. Directly adjacent to the [〜に隣接する] super luxury residential area [超高級住宅街] *Shōtō* is *Bunkamura*, an area

at the end of *Bunkamura-dōri* with a concert hall, museum, movie theater and the *Tōkyū* department store's <u>flagship location</u>. One can spend nearly an entire day in this
　　本店所在地

relaxed atmosphere, which stands <u>in sharp contrast to</u> the
　　　　　　　　　　　　　　　　　〜と際立って対照的に

bustling <u>vicinity</u> of *Shibuya* Station.
　　　　〜の周辺

---

72. 渋谷(しぶや)
エリアガイド

①ハチ公前スクランブル交差点は、今や海外からの旅行者にとって東京のシンボル的な場所となっています。街はそのハチ公前広場から、放射状に広がるイメージです。

②一番賑やかなのは、飲食店などがずらりと並ぶセンター街（通称バスケットボールストリート）と、それに並行する井(い)の頭(かしらどお)通りです。ファッションビルのSHIBUYA109から文化村通りを、デパートの渋谷西武方面に向かったこのエリアは、深夜まで人通りが絶えることがありません。

③大人の楽しめるエリアがあるのも、渋谷のいいところ。超高級住宅街・松濤(しょうとう)に隣接した文化村(ぶんかむら)通りの突き当りにあるBunkamuraは、コンサートホール、ミュージアム、映画館、東急百貨店本店などがあり、駅周辺とは対照的な落ち着いた雰囲気で一日を過ごせます。

73 *Shibuya* Station *Hachikō* Square
A dog loved by everyone

① American movie star Richard Gere was the lead actor in the well-known movie "*Hachi*: A Dog's Tale." This movie is based on the true story of an *Akita*-breed dog known as *Hachikō*, whose statue stands in front of the now famous Tokyo sightseeing spot that is the pedestrian scramble intersection in front of *Shibuya* Station's *Hachikō* exit.

② *Hachikō* was a dog that belonged to a University of Tokyo professor by the name of *Hidesaburō Ueno* in the early half of the 1920s, and every day the dog would come to *Shibuya* Station to await Professor *Ueno*'s return home. One day, however, Professor *Ueno* suddenly died while at work. *Hachikō* could not understand this of course and continued to return to the station at the usual time to wait for his master.

③ Eventually *Hachikō*'s 'devoted faithfulness to his master' became the subject of a newspaper article and people were

so <u>moved</u> that they held <u>a fundraising campaign</u> and col-
感動した　　　　　　　　　基金集めのイベント
lected money to build a statue of *Hachikō*, the faithful dog.
　　　　　　　　　　　　　　　　　　　　　　忠犬ハチ公

73. 渋谷駅ハチ公口前広場
今では皆の愛犬に

①アメリカの映画スター、リチャード・ギアが主演して話題になった映画「HACHI　約束の犬」。映画は、今や東京の観光名所である渋谷駅ハチ公口スクランブル交差点前に建つ忠犬ハチ公像のモデル、秋田犬のハチ公の逸話に基づいています。

②1920年代前半、東京大学教授・上野英三郎に飼われていたハチ公は、上野氏を毎日渋谷駅まで送り迎えしていましたが、ある日上野氏が学校で急逝。その事実を理解できなかったハチ公は、上野氏亡き後もじっと駅前でその帰りを待ち続けたのです。

③やがて新聞記事がきっかけで、ハチ公の「主人に忠義を尽くす」行いに感動した人々が、銅像建立基金集めのイベントまで行ってできたのが、忠犬ハチ公像です。

74

*SHIBUYA*109
The birthplace of girls' fashion

① Even now *SHIBUYA*109 remains at the very heart of girls' fashion. With over 120 stores specializing in everything from clothing to accessories as well as miscellaneous items, this area is always popular with teenagers and young women.

② There is an event space just outside the first floor entrance of the building's distinctive cylindrical front, and one can sometimes wander by and be surprised to see a well-known entertainer performing here.

---

74. SHIBUYA109
ガールズファッションの発信地

① ガールズファッション発信地といえば、今でもここSHIBUYA109でしょう。洋服にアクセサリー、雑貨など120店以上の店は、いつもティーンエイジャーをはじめ、若い女性で賑わっています。

② 外観が特徴的な建物の1階入り口前はイベントスペースになっており、「エッ」と驚くようなタレントが歌っていたりすることもあります。

75

Shibuya Hikarie
Shibuya's new symbolic tower

①This building along *Meiji-dōri* was built in combination
with the underground relocation of *Tōkyū Tōyoko* Line's
portion of *Shibuya* Station.

②As *Shibuya*'s new symbol tower, the building is home to a
full scale musical performance venue called the *Tōkyū Theater Orb*, in addition to unique and original restaurants,
(non-teenage) fashion and lifestyle shops.

75. 渋谷ヒカリエ
渋谷の新しいシンボルタワー

①明治通り沿いに、東急東横線渋谷駅地下化と相前後してできたビルです。
②本格派ミュージカル劇場の東急シアターオーブをはじめ、個性的なレストランや大人のファッションとライフスタイルの店が入る、渋谷の新しいシンボルタワーです。

76 AREA GUIDE

Omotesandō

①Rows of Japanese zelkova trees line the main street of the
ケヤキ
Omotesandō area from JR *Harajuku* Station to the
Omotesandō Subway Station (*Aoyama-dōri*).
　　地下鉄表参道駅
②The area in front of *Harajuku* Station has a casual
ambience with small shops selling sweets and other items.
雰囲気
However, the atmosphere of the streets leading to *Aoyama-*
　　　　　趣
dōri quickly changes, with a series of brand-name stores in
　　　　　　　　　　　　　　　　　　　ハイブランドの店
the center of the landmark *Omotesandō* Hills. A step further into the area's backstreets reveals numerous popular
　　　　　　　　裏通り
boutique fashion stores with their own distinctive styles.
ブティック　　　　　　　　　　　　　　個性的な
③An excellent spot to take photos is the pedestrian bridge
　　　　　　撮影スポット　　　　　　　歩道橋
just before the police box right as you are heading towards
　　　　　　交番　　　　　　　　　　　　　　　～へ向かう
Aoyama-dōri from *Meiji-dōri*. From the top of the bridge
　　　　　　　　　　　　　　　橋の上から
you can see a beautiful line of Japanese zelkova trees

extending <u>on both the left and right</u> that is more reminis-
　　　　　　　左右に　　　　　　　　　　　　　〜を思い出させる
cent of <u>a scene</u> in Paris or some other foreign cityscape
　　　　 風景
than somewhere in Japan.

76. 表参道
エリアガイド

①JR原宿駅から地下鉄表参道駅（青山通り）までのケヤキ並木が、表参道エリアのメインストリートです。

②原宿駅前周辺はちょっとしたスイーツなどを売るお店もあり、カジュアルな雰囲気。いっぽう青山通りへの通りはぐっと趣を変え、ランドマークの表参道ヒルズを中心にハイブランドの店が並びます。また一歩裏通りへ入ると、個性的なファッションで人気のブティックが軒を連ねています。

③おすすめの記念撮影スポットは明治通りから青山通りに向かう途中、交番の先にある歩道橋。歩道橋上から眺めた左右に延びる美しいケヤキ並木は、日本というよりパリかどこか外国の街並みを思わせます。

77. Meiji Jingū shrine

An oasis of fresh spring water in the metropolis

①This shrine was built in 1920 and dedicated to Emperor Meiji and Empress Shōken. A great number of people approach the shrine from its northern, southern and western entrances to worship at *hatsumōde* (the first visit to a temple or shrine just after the New Year begins).

②The highlight is the forest of trees along the approaches to the shrine that were gathered from all across Japan when the shrine was being constructed. There are large evergreen broadleaf trees such as chinquapin trees and oaks, among others.

---

77. 明治神宮
湧水もある都会のオアシス

①1920（大正9）年、明治天皇と昭憲皇太后をまつるために創建された神社です。正月の初詣では北・南・西のいずれの参道も、数多くの人で埋め尽くされます。
②見どころは、創建当時全国各地から献木され参道沿いに植樹された、椎や樫などの照葉樹の大木が生い茂る森です。

78 *Omotesandō* Hills
Refined buildings that retain an air of the past

①*Omotesandō* Hills is a landmark of *Omotesandō*. Internationally renowned architect *Tadao Andō* designed the fashion apparel building on the site of the *Dōjunkai Aoyama* Apartments housing complex.

②The shops inside the structure are inspired by the incline of *Omotesandō*'s main street as they are arranged somewhat unusually on a gentle slope that gradually spirals around each floor of the building, making this an enjoyable space for a stroll or casual window shopping.

---

78. 表参道ヒルズ
過去の記憶を留めるハイセンスな建物

①表参道のランドマークでもある、表参道ヒルズ。同潤会青山アパートの跡地に、国際的な建築家安藤忠雄の設計で建てられたファッションビルです。

②建物内の店舗は、建物内部を巡る螺旋状のスロープ沿いに並ぶ個性的な造りで、表参道の坂道を建物に取り込んでしまったような空間は、散策するだけでも楽しめます。

79 AREA GUIDE

Harajuku

①*Harajuku*'s development began around the same time as the current JR *Yamanote* Line's *Harajuku* Station was opened in 1906 and the *Meiji Jingū* shrine was constructed in 1920.

②After around 1958, one by one places at the forefront of luxury housing such as Central Apartment and Co-op Olympia were constructed and the area began to draw attention as a town where many famous people lived.

③Numerous stores targeted at young people now line *Meiji-dōri* towards the direction of *Yoyogi*, and the narrow backstreets also are filled with original boutique shops and cafes. On *Meiji-dōri* in the opposite direction towards *Shibuya*, famous brand stores stand side by side. The pedestrian path over the underground *Shibuya-gawa* River

that is commonly called Cat Street runs parallel to and
　　　通称〜と呼ばれる

eventually merges into *Meiji-dōri*, and with new boutique

shops and restaurants constantly opening, this is an excit-

ing promenade that captures the essence of *Harajuku*.
　　散歩道

79. 原宿
エリアガイド

①原宿が発展を始めたのは、現在のJR山手線原宿駅の1906（明治39）年の開業と、1920（大正9）年の明治神宮創建の頃からです。

②1958（昭和33）年頃から、高級賃貸住宅の先駆け的なセントラルアパートやコープオリンピアなどが次々と造られ、有名人などが多く住む町として注目を集めるようになりました。

③現在、代々木方面に向かう明治通り沿いは若い人向けの店が立ち並び、細い裏通りに沿いにも個性的なブティックやカフェなどがあります。反対側の渋谷へ向かう明治通り沿いには、有名ブランドの店が並びます。また、明治通りと並行し最終的には合流する渋谷川暗渠の遊歩道は、通称キャットストリートと呼ばれ、次々と新しいブティックや飲食店がオープン、格好の散歩道になっています。

80 *Takeshita-dōri* Street
Sacred ground for teenagers

①*Takeshita-dōri* is filled with hordes of teenagers on weekends and holidays. Boutique shops and stores selling accessories line this small street which is also a draw for many foreign tourists. About 300 meters from JR *Harajuku* Station heading towards *Meiji-dōri*, this area started changing into a street for smart fashion around the mid-1970s when the Palais France building opened. Import record specialist stores, boutiques, and accessory shops opened one after another and with the emergence of *Takenoko-zoku* dance groups in the early half of the 1980s, the street became a teenage fashion Mecca.

②Heading out of JR *Harajuku* Station's *Takeshita* exit toward *Meiji-dōri*, stores decked out in gaudy colors such as pink and red catch the eye.

③Turning left about halfway down the narrow street towards *Meiji-dōri*, you will immediately enter the pre-

cincts of *Tōgō-jinja* shrine. Dense with sacred tall trees in
東郷神社
the grove of a village shrine, this is an oasis of tranquility
鎮守の森   静けさ
that stands in contrast to the bustle of

Takeshita-dōri.

80. 竹下通り
ティーンエイジャーの聖地

①休日ともなれば、ティーンエイジャーで埋め尽くされる竹下通り。小物の店やブティックが建ち並び、外国人観光客も多く見られます。JR原宿駅から明治通りに向かう300mほどのこの裏通りは、1970年代半ばのパレフランスビルのオープンで、ちょっとおしゃな大人の街として変身し始めます。輸入盤レコード専門店やブティック、雑貨店などが次々とオープン、さらに1980年代前半、竹の子族の出現で、ティーンエイジャーファッションのメッカとなっていきました。

②JR原宿駅竹下口を出て明治通りに向かっていくと、ピンク色や赤などの派手な色使いの店が目に飛び込んできます。

③明治通りに向かって通りの中ほどをちょっと左へ入ると、そこはもう東郷神社の境内。ご神木の大木が生い茂る鎮守の森は、竹下通りとは対照的に静謐な空間を造っています。

Nō plays 能楽(のうがく)

Nō is one of Japan's traditional performing arts. Performers wear a mask and recite their lines in a unique form of intonation known as *utai*. The *nō* stage is basically comprised of performers called *shite* and *waki*, in combination with instrumentalists called *hayashikata* who play *ōtsuzumi* (hip drum), *kotsuzumi* (shoulder-drum), *fue* (transverse flute), and *taiko* (stick-drum), together with a chorus called *jiutai*.

With the support of the shogun *Ashikaga Yoshimitsu* who wielded tremendous power in the 14th century's *Namboku-chō* period, *Kan'ami* and his son *Zeami* combined elements of various other arts with the period's *yamato sarugaku* entertainments, culminating in what is described today as *nō*. In particular it is said that *Zeami* helped establish the *mugen nō* (phantasm *nō*) production technique that is connected to modern day performances centered on the *shite* role.

Although *sarugaku* was well received by the common people throughout the *Muromachi* period, when the weakening of the *Muromachi Bakufu* government ushered in the *Sengoku* or Warring States period, *nō* practitioners relied on the support of regional feudal lords or *daimyō* and began to draw away from *Kyōto*. *Oda Nobunaga*, the supreme ruler during the Warring States period, and his successor, *Toyotomi Hidetoshi*, greatly enjoyed *nō*. The four schools of *yamato sarugaku* that are connected to the current *Kanze*, *Hōshō*, *Kongō*, and *Komparu* schools received direct support under *Toyotomi's* administration. It is said that present day *nō* masks, clothing and stage format, etc. were determined by influence of the splendid *Azuchi-Momoyama* culture in the final phase of the

旅のポイント

Warring States period.

Now in addition to regular public performances of *nō* and *Kyōgen* (a farce presented between *nō* plays) at the *Kokuritsu Nō-gakudō* (National *Nō* Theater) in *Shibuya* ward's *Sendagaya* area, there are also public performances of the different *nō* schools at *nō* theaters around the city such as the *Ginza Nō-gakudō* and the *Yarai Nō-gakudō*.

能面をつけ、謡といわれる独特の節回しで台詞を朗誦する日本の伝統芸能です。舞台は、基本的にシテとワキと呼ばれる演者により演じられ、ほかに大鼓、小鼓、笛、太鼓の囃子方と地謡で構成されます。

14世紀の南北朝時代に絶大な権力を誇った将軍足利義満の支援のもと、観阿弥・世阿弥親子によって当時の「大和猿楽」は、他のさまざまな芸能の要素を取り込みながら「能」という表現に集大成されていきます。とくに世阿弥の代に、現在につながるシテを中心とする「夢幻能」演出手法が確立したと伝えられます。

さらに室町時代を通じて猿楽は庶民にも受け入れられていきますが、室町幕府の弱体化により戦国時代に入ったことで、能楽師たちは地方の有力大名を頼りに、京都を離れ始めます。なかでも戦国時代の覇者である織田信長やその後継者である豊臣秀吉が能楽を好み、豊臣政権下、現在の観世・宝生・金剛・金春につながる大和猿楽四座が直接庇護されました。絢爛豪華な安土桃山文化の影響で、現在の能面、衣装、舞台形式などが定まったといわれます。

現在、渋谷区千駄ヶ谷に国立能楽堂があり、能・狂言の定例公演が行われているほか、銀座能楽堂、矢来能楽堂など都内各所の能楽堂で各流派の公演が行われています。

81 AREA GUIDE
Ebisu, Daikan'yama

①In 1889, the Japan Beer Brewery Company's (now *Sapporo* Beer) factory was built to produce and sell '*Yebisu* Beer.' A railroad freight station was created at *Ebisu* in 1901, and a few years later passenger trains started stopping at the station as well. The '*Ebisu*' name was given to the surrounding neighborhood in the latter half of the 1920s.

②The town expanded as a station for both the JR *Yamanote* Line and the *Hibiya* Subway Line, and after *Yebisu* Garden Place was opened and JR *Ebisu* Station was remodeled, upscale restaurants and bars began increasing in number during the *Heisei* period (the last 25 years or so) and the area is now a town that is fashionable among adults.

③Located about 15 minutes by foot from *Ebisu* is the *Tōkyū*

第4章●東京の繁華街

Tōyoko Line's *Daikan'yama* Station. *Daikan'yama* area is
<u>東急東横線</u>
characterized by fashionable boutique shops and accessory
<u>〜が特徴の</u>
stores as well as restaurants and bars.

81. 恵比寿・代官山
エリアガイド

① 1889（明治22）年、現在のサッポロビールの前身である日本麦酒醸造会社の工場が造られ、「エビスビール」が売り出されました。1901（明治34）年に鉄道の貨物駅・恵比寿停車場ができ、数年後から旅客列車も停車するようになります。1920年代後半、付近の町名が「恵比寿」と名付けられて現在に至ります。
② JR山手線と地下鉄日比谷線恵比寿駅を中心に広がる街並みは、恵比寿ガーデンプレイスのオープンと、それに伴うJR恵比寿駅の改築で、平成以降ハイセンスな飲食店などが増え始め、現在ではちょっとしゃれた大人の街となっています。
③ 恵比寿からは徒歩15分ほどのところに位置する、東急東横線代官山駅。この代官山周辺は、おしゃれなブティック・雑貨店や飲食店が特徴のこぢんまりとした街です。

82 *Yebisu* Garden Place
Experience the taste and history of Japanese beer

①The *Sapporo* beer factory location that had existed since the *Meiji* period was redeveloped, giving birth to the *Yebisu* Garden Place. With the 40-story *Yebisu* Garden Place Tower at its heart, this extensive complex includes office space, the *Mitsukoshi* department store's *Ebisu* branch, the Tokyo Metropolitan Museum of Photography, the *Sapporo* Beer Station beer hall, and the Westin Hotel Tokyo.

②If you like beer, head over to the Museum of *Yebisu* Beer where you can sample *Yebisu* Beer while learning about its history. Of course, you can also enjoy some beers at the 'Beer Station' or the '*Ginza* Lion' beer hall.

③For a little luxury, try the finest French cuisine at Joël Robuchon Restaurant, which has acquired three Michelin Tokyo stars. Or there is also La Table de Joël Robuchon, where you can try modern French food in a more casual

setting. This restaurant has also secured two stars in the
環境　　　　　　　　　　　　　　　　　獲得した
Michelin Tokyo rankings.

82. 恵比寿ガーデンプレイス
日本のビールの歴史と味を堪能

①明治時代以降サッポロビール工場のあった場所が再開発され、誕生したのが恵比寿ガーデンプレイスです。40階建の恵比寿ガーデンプレイスタワーを核に、オフィス、百貨店の恵比寿三越、東京都写真美術館、ビアホールのサッポロビヤステーション、ウェスティンホテル東京などがある複合都市です。

②ビール好きなら、ヱビスビール記念館へ。ヱビスビールの歴史を知りながらテイスティングができます。もちろんビアホールの「ビアステーション」や、「銀座ライオン」でもビールが楽しめます。

③ちょっと贅沢をしたかったらミシュラン東京で三ツ星を獲得したレストラン「ガストロノミー　ジョエル・ロブション」で、最高峰のフランス料理を。いっぽう「ラ・ターブル　ドゥ　ジョエル・ロブション」では、カジュアルにモダン・フレンチを味わえます。こちらもミシュラン東京で二つ星を獲得しています。

83 AREA GUIDE

Kichijōji

① *Kichijōji* is said to be the most desirable place to live in
　　　　　　　　　　　　　住みたい街ナンバーワン
Tokyo. It has become an even more convenient town due to
　　　　　　　　　　　　ますます
the consecutive renewal over the past two years of two
　　　連続した　　　　　　　ここ2年
major shopping facilities that are adjacent to the train sta-
　　　　　　　　　　　　　　　～に隣接した
tion, Atre *Kichijōji* and the new station building *Kirarina*.
　　　アトレ吉祥寺
② *Kichijōji* is a compact town, yet there is an abundant
　　　　　　　　　　　　　　　　　　　バラエティ豊かな
variety of shops filling the area from the station vicinity to
　　　　　　　　　　　　　　　　　　駅周辺
the main roads of *Inokashira-dōri* and *Itsukaichi-kaidō*.
Both the Sun Road and *Daiya-gai* shopping arcades are
　　　　　　　　　　　　　　　　　　　アーケードモール
covered so you can enjoy strolling around them even on
　　　　　　　　　　　　　　散策する
rainy days.

③ A local market opened after the Pacific War, and a trace
　　　　　　　　　　　　　　　　　　　　　　　　　面影
of one part of that original market can be found in the pres-
　　　　　　　　　　　　　　　　　　～を見ることができる
ent Harmonica *Yokochō*. Since the *Shōwa* period's 40s (the
　　　ハモニカ横丁　　　　　　　　　　昭和

mid-1960s to mid-1970s), department stores such as *Isetan* (now Coppice *Kichijōji*), *Kintetsu* (now *Yodobashi Camera*), and *Tōkyū* opened consecutively, and the area became popular as an easily accessible shopping town from the Tokyo metropolis, with throngs of shoppers turning out on the weekends.

---

83. 吉祥寺
エリアガイド

①東京で住みたい街ナンバーワンといわれる吉祥寺。ここ２年ほどで以前からあった駅に隣接したショッピング施設が、アトレ吉祥寺と新駅ビルのキラリナに相次いでリニューアルされ、ますます便利な街になりました。

②コンパクトな街ながら、駅周辺から井の頭通り周辺と五日市街道沿いまでバラエティ豊かなお店が広がっており、サンロードとダイヤ街はいずれもアーケードモールなので、雨の日でも散策を楽しめます。

③太平洋戦争後はマーケットが開かれ、その一部が現在もハモニカ横丁にその面影を伝えています。昭和40年代以降は、伊勢丹（現・コピス吉祥寺）、近鉄（現・ヨドバシカメラ）、東急など次々とデパートがオープンし、首都圏近郊のショッピングタウンとして週末には多くの買い物客で賑わいます。

84 *Inokashira Onshi* Park
A river source in the metropolis, surrounded by lush greenery

①The fresh spring that feeds *Inokashira* Pond in the center of *Inokashira* Park is the source of the *Kanda-gawa* River which runs from west to east within Tokyo and merges into the larger *Sumida-gawa* River. From the *Edo* period to the late *Meiji* period, this pond water known as *Kanda jōsui* supported the water supply needs of the city's population.

In 1913, *Inokashira* Park became Japan's first suburban park and along with the adjacent *Goten'yama* area's natural forest and the *Inokashira* Park Zoo it is still a popular place for city folk to rest and relax.

②In spring a large number of people who come to view the beautiful blossoms on the cherry trees that ring the sides of the pond. We recommend renting one of the small boats available and viewing the cherry blossoms from the water. The branches of the cherry trees hang low, almost touching the surface of the water. You can pass underneath the

branches. In the fall, the changing leaves of <u>the Japanese</u>
<u>maples</u> and other trees planted here are a popular <u>sight</u>.
　　　　　　　　　　　　　　　　　　　　　　　　　　　　カエデ　　　　　　　　　　　　　　　　　　　　　　　　見もの
③There are small tea shops throughout the park which
offer light meals and alcoholic drinks.
〜を提供する

84. 井の頭恩賜公園
緑豊かな都会の水源

①都内を西から東へ流れ、隅田川へと注ぐ神田川の源流が、井の頭恩賜公園の中央にある井の頭池の湧水です。江戸時代から明治後期まで、この池の水は神田上水として人々の生活を支えていました。1913（大正2）年に日本最初の郊外型公園として整備され、今でも隣接する御殿山の自然林と井の頭自然文化園とともに、都民の憩いの場になっています。

②春には、池をぐるりと囲むように植えられた桜のお花見スポットとして大変な賑わいを見せます。おすすめはボートに乗って眺める、水上からのお花見。桜の枝が池の水面すれすれまで張り出して、その下をくぐることができます。秋には数多く植えられたカエデなどの木々の紅葉も楽しめます。

③園内各所に茶店があり、軽食やお酒も楽しめます。

85

Harmonica *Yokochō*
Lose yourself in a *Shōwa*-period market

①Harmonica *Yokochō* (Harmonica alley) is a corner of town (〜の一角) in front of JR *Kichijōji* Station's north exit (北口) that preserves (〜を保つ) the area's market atmosphere (たたずまい) from just after the war.
②From the 1990s, *izakaya* (Japanese pubs) that were attractive to young people slowly increased in number (数が増えた) and now the area is gaining popularity (人気を集めている) as a place to bring family (家族を連れて行く) and get a taste of nostalgia (昔懐かしい趣) for the *Shōwa* (昭和) period.

---

85. ハモニカ横丁
昭和の市場に迷い込もう

①JR吉祥寺駅北口前の一角、戦後間もない頃のマーケットのたたずまいそのままに残るのが、ハモニカ横丁です。
②90年代に入って若者でも入りやすい居酒屋が徐々に増え、現在は家族連れでも古き懐かしき昭和を味わえる一角として人気を集めています。

第4章●東京の繁華街

86 Atre *Kichijōji*, Kirarina *Kichijōji*
A shopping paradise in the new station building

①Directly below the JR *Kichijōji* Station platforms is Atre
　～の真下に　　　　　　　　　　　　　　　　　　　ホーム

Kichijōji, a long shopping mall extending from east to west
　　　　　　　　　　　　　　　　　　　　　　東西に

with two stories above ground and one floor underground
　　　　　　　　　　地上　　　　　　　　　　　　地下

that used to be called Lonlon.
　かつて～と呼ばれていた

②The building above the *Keiō Inokashira* Line's *Kichijōji*
　　　　　　　　　　　京王井の頭線

Station well known as Terminal Echo was completely

rebuilt and reborn as *Kirarina Kichijōji* in 2014.
　　　　　～に生まれ変わった

---

86. アトレ吉祥寺・キラリナ吉祥寺
新駅ビルでショッピング三昧

①JR吉祥寺駅のホーム下に地上2階地下1階で東西に長ーく伸びるのが、かつて「ロンロン」と呼ばれていたショッピングモールのアトレ吉祥寺です。
②また「ターミナル・エコー」の名前で親しまれていた京王井の頭線吉祥寺駅上ビルが全面的に建て替えられ、2014（平成26）年にキラリナ吉祥寺に生まれ変わりました。

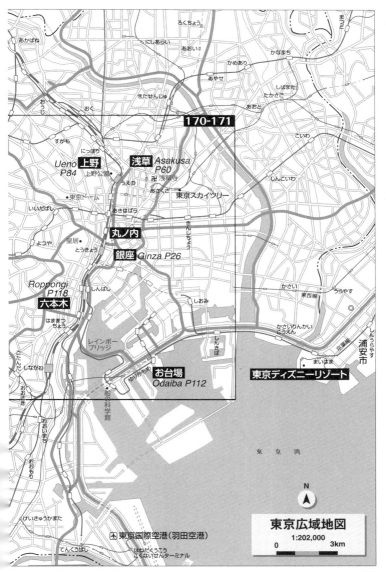

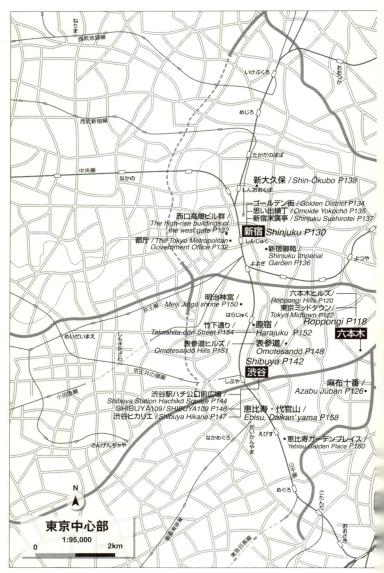

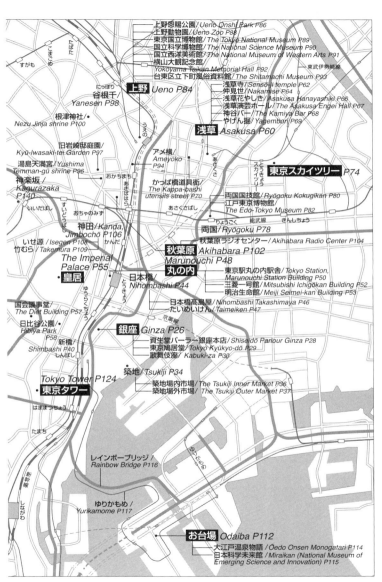

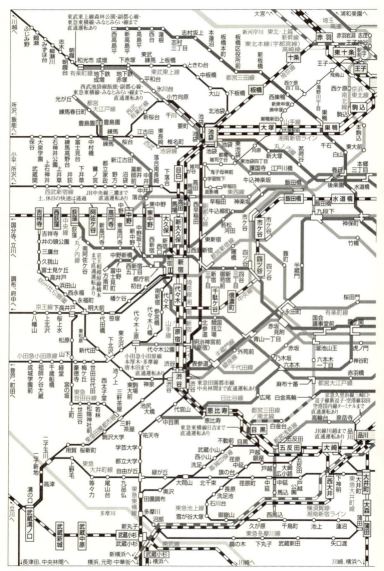

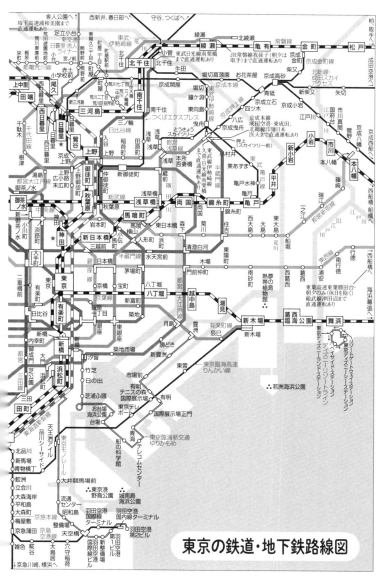

≪参考文献≫

『オタク論!』唐沢 俊一・岡田 斗司夫著（創出版）
『古地図で謎解き 江戸東京「まち」の歴史』跡部 蛮著（双葉社）
『スーパービジュアル版　江戸・東京の地理と地名』鈴木理生著（日本実業出版）
『地図と写真から見える！江戸・東京　歴史を楽しむ』南谷果林著（西東社）
『東京の歴史地図帳』谷川彰英著（宝島社）

≪参考ウェブサイト≫

居酒屋の楽しみ方……http://www.izakaya-hanamaru.com/
歌舞伎座……http://www.kabuki-za.co.jp/
鳩居堂……http://www.kyukyodo.co.jp/
Ginza Official－銀座公式ウェブサイト……http://www.ginza.jp/
宮内庁……http://www.kunaicho.go.jp/
資生堂パーラー……http://parlour.shiseido.co.jp/index.html
たいめいけん……http://www.taimeiken.co.jp/
日本橋タカシマヤ……http://www.takashimaya.co.jp/tokyo/
中央区観光協会……http://www.chuo-kanko.or.jp/
築地場外市場……http://www.tsukiji.or.jp/
東京都中央卸売市場……http://www.shijou.metro.tokyo.jp/
東京の観光公式サイトGO TOKYO……http://www.gotokyo.org/jp/
日本文化いろは辞典……http://iroha-japan.net/
文化庁……http://www.bunka.go.jp/
三菱一号館……http://mitsubishi-ichigokan.jp/
明治安田生命……http://www.meijiyasuda.co.jp/

英文翻訳者

Jon Morris（ジョン・モリス）
英国北ヨークシャー出身。
ブリストル大学学士課程、哲学、神学と宗教学専攻卒業後、2001年から2004年まで島根県立浜田商業高校で助手英語教師を務める。
2005年ロンドン大学東洋アフリカ研究学院、修士課程、仏教学専攻を卒業。
2010年東北大学大学院、博士前期課程、日本思想史専攻卒業後、後期課程に進学。
現在は東北学院大学と尚絅学院大学で非常勤講師を務めながら、翻訳者、研究者として活動している。

じっぴコンパクト新書　239

楽しく歩ける！楽々わかる！
英語対訳で旅する東京
Travel in Tokyo with simple English

2015年2月5日　初版第1刷発行

編　集	ブルーガイド編集部
発行者	村山秀夫
発行所	実業之日本社
	〒104-8233　東京都中央区京橋3-7-5　京橋スクエア
	電話(編集) 03-3535-5411
	(販売) 03-3535-4441
	http://www.j-n.co.jp/
印刷所	大日本印刷株式会社
製本所	株式会社ブックアート

©Jitsugyo No Nihon Sha,Ltd.2015, Printed in Japan
ISBN978-4-408-00867-7（ブルーガイド出版部）
落丁・乱丁の場合は小社でお取り替えいたします。
実業之日本社のプライバシー・ポリシー（個人情報の取扱い）は、上記サイトをご覧ください。
本書の一部あるいは全部を無断で複写・複製（コピー、スキャン、デジタル化等）・転載することは、法律で認められた場合を除き、禁じられています。
また、購入者以外の第三者による本書のいかなる電子複製も一切認められておりません。